THE LOGIC OF
SOCIAL INQUIRY

THE LOGIC OF SOCIAL INQUIRY

SCOTT GREER
NORTHWESTERN UNIVERSITY

ALDINE PUBLISHING COMPANY

CHICAGO

"The Death of the Ball-Turret Gunner" reprinted with the per-
mission of Farrar, Straus, & Girout, Inc. from *Little Friend, Little
Friend* by Randall Jarrell, Copyright 1945 by Mrs. Randall Jarrell.
"Strokes" from *The Rescued Years* by William Stafford. Copyright
© 1956 by William Stafford. Reprinted by permission of Harper &
Row, Publishers.

"The Third Culture and the Self-Fulfilling Prophecy," was first
published in *Tri-Quarterly*.

The figure on p. 102 is reprinted from Wendell Bell's "The Social
Areas of the San Francisco Bay Region," *American Sociological Re-
view*, February 1953, by permission of the University of Chicago
Press.

First published 1969 by Aldine Publishing Company
529 South Wabash, Chicago, Illinois 60605

Library of Congress Catalog 68-8150

Designed by Chestnut House

*This book is dedicated
to my teacher John James
who helped me begin it, and
to my student Ann Lennarson
who helped me complete it.*

PREFACE

In this volume I have tried to formulate clearly what the enterprise of social science looks like to one practitioner. As a sociologist whose primary concern is with social organization, I do not consider myself to be a logician, philosopher of science, mathematician, or (except in the broadest sense) a methodologist. I am a working social scientist and teacher, and I want to show both the relevance of the broadest philosophical questions to the research scientist and the relevance of his work to major questions concerning the human situation.

It is well to remember that all of the sciences evolved from one mother, philosophy. For us to understand their significance all must finally be related to that parentage: in this sense all scientists are philosophers. But so great has been the proliferation of knowledge, so complexly specialized our achievement, that the great root of meaning has long been lost to the sight of many of us. This context of significance, which alone gives meaning to the social sciences, is often vulgarized, assumed or, worse, forgotten.

Thus the student, the neophyte scientist, the interested common reader, often comes to social science with confusion and may harvest only a small order among a great disorder. He asks of science what it cannot, in its nature, give: he rejects what is possible. The problem lies as deep as the fragmentation of our culture; it results in a mindless antiscientism on the part of some intellectuals at one extreme, a blind faith in science on the part of the semiliterate at the other. C. P. Snow has argued that we are "two cultures," the scientific and the humanistic. I think this argument itself proof of barbarism within our intellectual gates, for the most important culture of all, social science, is ignored. Yet it alone is capable of bridging the distance between nuclear physics and literary criticism, for its aim is to provide a basic calculus for understanding the socially generated significance of both.

I have emphasized the essentially creative in social science, the generation of concept and theory, the transformations of our symbolic map of society. The reader will note my debt to Alfred North Whitehead, for me one of the most creative men ever to write, and to his student Suzanne Langer. Both address the most important moot issue in the philosophy of social science (and in our training of social scientists) —conceptual creativity. Our literature on methods devotes hundreds of pages to the rules for testing concepts, few or none to the generation of them. I do not accept that council of despair which simply relies on the mysticism of individual greatness to explain such matters: I think we can do better than that. To omit concern for the formation of concepts from a treatment of social science is to present a false picture, one which, taken literally, would give a self-respecting intellect no reason to demean itself by working in social science.

This would be a pity for social science is the most important intellectual enterprise of the day. If we are to destroy ourselves with thermonuclear devices it will be the fault not of the physicist but of the social actors who run our society and the vision of the world that informs their actions. Thus while my major concern is with the development of a true, empirically powerful social science, I am also concerned with the complex interaction of social science and social policy.

Ethics, esthetics, and science are frequently discussed as three utterly separate domains. Conflict among our intellectual formulations of these major aspects of experience is the root cause of the cultural schizophrenia that Snow addresses. In sketching my own solution, my notion of an appropriate way to relate them, I have been motivated by my commitment to the arts and to the human community. And, I might add,

much inspired by the obvious concern of the young social
scientists with whom I have discussed these matters for the
past decade. Too often they have seen social science as requiring the great abnegation, a choice that forecloses concern
with the values of social action and the arts. Having experienced similar strain during my own apprenticeship to rigorous,
disciplined inquiry, I know that the death of such desire is
entirely unnecessary. For I believe the high cool abstraction
created in the vise of hard fact is not only the best tool for
social action; it is also the most useful ground for those symbolic creations through which we celebrate human life in the
world.

CONTENTS

xi

[I]

THE SCIENTIFIC POSITION

[1]

SCIENCE AS SOCIAL ACTION

As attending to art begins with "the willing suspension of disbelief," social science starts with a willed suspension of belief. In the ordinary business of living we are accustomed to accept on faith a fantastically complex set of assumptions about the social world and the actors in it; this is what is meant by "culture." The social scientist, reversing Hamlet, always suspects that "there are more things in your philosophy than Heaven and Earth have dreamed of." In short, he rejects the culture's typical assumptions, or holds them in mind only tentatively while requiring they show cause to be included as propositions in the body of his knowledge. Against them he erects counter-propositions and spins new networks of meaning for social life.

This is a difficult and devious mode of existence. For in ordinary action, including discourse, his fellow men are filled with trust, however misplaced, while he is the epitome of distrust (however misplaced) in what is called conventional wisdom, or folk thought. And being less than logically perfect, all social scientists apply the rule of scepticism with some degree of bias; at an extreme, they stand upon one questionable assumption in order to get leverage for toppling a dozen others. In short, we are always in danger of solipsism. It is for this reason that we have evolved a certain process that results in making those propositions we are willing to allow a probationary residence in our science.

This process may best be thought of as circular. If we are lucky and our scientific knowledge accumulates, it may spiral upward; it may also revolve at the same level, a merry-go-

3

round of fashion; or it may spiral downward, from theory to doctrine to dogma. In any event, the basic process of inquiry runs this circular course: (1) In the beginning is the problem. The scientist is a man with a problem or he is nothing. (2) The problem is conceptualized in such a way to suggest a trial solution. A "model" or "mock-up" is constructed in the mind, one that places the problem in a larger frame of reference. (3) The trial solution is tested, logically and empirically. Logically we look for vagueness, evasion, internal contradictions, or conflict with what is already definitely known. Empirically, we deduce from the mock-up what should be the case in the world we experience, and then go out to see if our experiences jibe with the deductions: i.e., we predict what we will find in the world outside our speculation and deductions. (4) We then evaluate our test results against what we had expected. We also evaluate our test procedure—our attitude scales or demographic measures or what have you—asking if they were a fair test of the deduced hypothesis. (While a test can negate a proposition, remember that the reverse also holds: the failure of the theory may simply reflect the inadequacy of the testing procedure.) (5) Finally, the results of this problem solving are used to readjust the framework in which the test was couched. Failure or success equally point to extending and editing theory. The revised frame of reference gives birth, in turn, to new and unforeseen "problems."

This is a brief and perhaps cryptic sketch of the "research cycle," the process of inquiry. It will be expanded through the remainder of this volume, but let it stand, for now, as a paradigm of scientific inquiry. It immediately raises an important question: how does such a procedure protect us from those many things in our philosophy that "the world" has not even dreamed of? The very integrity of social science depends upon the answer. When each is an interested party in the game of social life, when our mind is half immobilized in the swaddling clothes of culture, how is it possible for us to deal objectively with anything as vital as the problems of race conflict, sex roles, economic futures, and world wars?

Karl Mannheim, writing of *Ideology and Utopia,* proposed one answer.* In the chaotic and frightening period between two world wars, intellectual and political discourse was confused and abused by the proponents of various ideologies— which were given greater strength by a basic despair of any possible objectivity. On the one hand the leftists, taking their lead from the shrewd insights of Karl Marx, argued that most "bourgeois" social science was merely ideology, apologetics for the existing capitalist society. For the Marxist, action was not the result of thought; instead, as a man was, so would he think. His relationship to the means of production as entrepreneur, financier, employee, would in the long run determine his thinking. Thus his version of "truth" would always be a defense of his position in the economic order. The fascists, relying on a blood mystique and a theory of historical inevitability, came to the same conclusion with different categories; for them, thought and action were both the product of one's race and "blood." Thus communism was a "Jewish conspiracy" to fascists, while fascism was a "last reflex of the dying capitalist system" to communists. In such a world, all hope of objectivity seemed lost.

Mannheim saw the larger truth: men are always in danger of powerful biases growing out of their ways of life and the differences among them. All visions of society require a perspective and that perspective will be much affected by one's position in the world. How then do we find a unifying perspective? For Mannheim the answer was the development of habitually objective thinkers. These, in turn, were people who had experienced a variety of perspectives on similar events. Implicit here is Simmel's notion of *marginality.* Though we exist in social circles that are coercive and subtly decisive for our ways of thought, some of us exist where many circles overlap: on the margins of many groups, we share many different and often contradictory assumptions. We are then forced to arbitrate differences which the various groups we know can

* All references and notes will be found at the back of the book, starting on page 207

ignore, since they do not have to confront each other in serious and intimate discourse. Thus the dialectic of social thought plays itself out within the marginal and (intellectually) lonely individual. Such individuals are the seedgrounds for objective knowledge, transcending the various dogmas and folklores of the natural interest groups human society continually creates.

Mannheim's answer, however ingenious, does not really solve the problem. It points to the kinds of individuals who may have socially detached perspectives (within the limits of their larger cultural horizons), but it does not tell us how to arbitrate the objective quality of their thinking. Nor, further, does it allow us to discriminate between objectivity and accuracy: one may be just as objective in error as in truth. He tells us what kinds of situation may produce hypotheses transcending the folk thought and interests of specific groups within the society; he does not tell us how to judge them for their usefulness as maps of the world.

For the social scientist, such judgment is possible only within a community that shares basic aims and the rules for achieving those aims. The individual, however brilliant and detached, is always subordinate to the community's evaluation of the kind and quality of work he produces. In short, Mannheim's *ad hominem* approach to scientific validity is a trap not too different from the Marxist and fascist traps. It fastens on social structure as such, but omits consideration for the social structure of knowledge. Yet in that structure is, finally, the only guarantee of scientific validity.

The structure is diverse and complex. Let us simplify, however, by emphasizing the two major norms that underlie all the others. They are, interestingly, procedural norms; they do not tell us anything about the substance of our propositions or beliefs, but merely how they may be socially established. They are continual controls upon our innate propensity to create new versions of the world with questionable relations to reality. Yet because they are procedural they are open, infinitely tolerant of new idea and fact.

The first of these norms is simply *the norm of publicity*.

Individual operations, whether they are speculative and logical, or empirically descriptive, must be open to group surveillance—a jury of one's peers. This is the reason for the fantastic proliferation of professional societies, professional journals, symposia, and meetings. For the social scientist, the true creation of science occurs only when he makes public his work. As the entire research cycle is evaluated, his work has its chance to become a part of that social fact called "social science." It is also possible for his colleagues to replicate his work, with test results that support or challenge his findings.

This process brings up another control on inquiry: *the constant reversibility of decisions*. No specific issue is ever closed "once and for all." To be sure it may be generally assumed for centuries, as with Newton's model of the physical universe, but it is always in principle modifiable by an Einstein. This is another way of saying that scientific knowledge is perpetually hypothetical in nature: at any one point in history it amounts to humanity's best guess about the nature of things.

That best guess may be deplorably wrong. It is a depressing fact that racism was strongly reinforced, if not originated, by social scientists in the nineteenth century. The "inferiority" of certain races was widely assumed, and indeed early research on racial differences was frequently a documentation of such ideas. As, however, the research cycle became a general part of social scientific inquiry, the very studies aimed at showing racial differences came increasingly to contradict such assumptions. The first mass of adequate data, collected in the United States during the military draft for World War I, produced such erratic and contradictory data that race as a major explanatory tool, independent of culture, was never again respectable in American social science. Thus the fallacious "best guess," exposed to the rigors of the research cycle, could be replaced by the more accurate (and interesting) theories current today.

The norm of publicity and the norm of reversibility protect the research cycle from irrelevant authority and individ-

ual chicanery. Neither can be waived without serious dangers
to the collective enterprise of social science. They are not sufficient conditions for the development of a powerful science,
but they are necessary. Biology cannot be made by Soviet
commissars, however great their ideological need, just as
demography could not be made by Hitler or Mussolini when
they pleaded population expansion as the basis for demanding
more "living space." Outside the pressure cooker of policy-
making, outside the nation state, is a larger scientific community which must be shown—not harangued.

ON THE SELECTION OF PROBLEMS

Science as intellectual innovation of a specific kind represents
finding and solving problems. And the nature of the problem,
the way it is posed, determines the kind of solution possible;
problem selection is a major part of social inquiry. Curiously
enough, there is little real agreement on "problematics"; indeed, the question is muted in the literature of social science
methodology. Yet it is very important to distinguish between
the kinds of problematic situations that give rise to inquiry,
for their fruits vary consistently.

Let us begin with the scientist as an actor within a setting,
for both actor and setting are necessary to produce a problematic situation. The setting is one in which those aspects that
concern the actor are not fully defined. (It is important to remember that only some aspects of a situation are of any
concern to any one actor.) Some aspects are presumed to be
clearly known, but others are indeterminate—unknown. The
actor faces first a problem of intellectual definition.

Resolution of the problematic situation may come about in
many ways. These include religion ("trust in God") and
other styles of rejecting the problem, from fatalism to suppression of the disturbing unknown. More specifically, resolution may come about in rationalistic ways, by taking thought

and subsuming the problematic situation under general regularities already known, or inventing new kinds of regularities that may not have been propounded before.

These resolutions, rational though they are, need not be scientific. The intellectual history of mankind is littered with the pseudosciences, from astrology to palmistry. And historically theological explanations have been an important form of rationalism; they explain the given instant of mystery through assumptions about the ultimate purposes of God or the gods in history and the world. To be scientific, the resolution of the problem must follow the research cycle; to be adequately scientific it must follow rather rigorously certain rules that will be discussed later. But prior to the resolution, the question: where do the problems of social science come from?

There seem to be at least three broad classes of problematic situations that give rise to social inquiry. Each grows out of change and resulting conflict, and each remains important in contemporary research in the social sciences. They may be grouped under three labels: policy problems; problems of social philosophy; and problems intrinsic to developing scientific disciplines.

The policy problem was the first sort to be attacked empirically, for its resolution must be in empirically testable terms. It is the problem of everyday life in the society, a problem of practical urgency. Its salience is clear in the general concern with social and clinical problems and the industries (social welfare, psychiatry) that have emerged to deal with them. Much of the public acceptance of the social sciences today comes from the average citizen's concern with poverty, race relations, mental illness, and crime.

Such problems are always defined by the *values* of the society. Growing out of value conflict, they represent efforts to reformulate the world and bring it closer to what is desired. At an extreme, policy problems represent the impulse symbolized in a speech from a play by Dennis Johnston: "I will take this world between my two hands and batter it into the symbol of my heart's desire." Such a problematic situation evokes no need for general knowledge, other than that which allows us to intervene with confidence in the stream of things, diverting it in directions we prefer.

Policy problems emerge from the discrepancy between the ideal and the actual and signal overt conflict between them. This may be conflict within the group, as in our present concern with the rights and duties of Negro citizens in the United States; it may be conflict between the values of the group and the nature of the environment, as in the gap between the rising aspirations of the new nations and their economic poverty; it may be conflict between groups, as in the tension between the two major thermonuclear powers in the world today. In any case, it is a dramatic difference between what the actor believes desirable and what he thinks exists that triggers the policy problem.

It is in such terms that it must be solved. The goal is to move actuality, as seen by the problem-definer, toward his ideal state of things. Negroes achieve rights and duties acceptable to the working consensus; the rate of economic activity rises at the same speed as rising aspirations; Russia and the United States achieve a *détente*. The focus of social inquiry into policy problems is upon clues to manipulation and action.

But note carefully that the policy problem is an abstraction from a very complex social situation. There are, after all, many other striking and intriguing aspects of minority-majority relations, of the specific ways of life among Negroes and whites or the change of simple into urban societies, that are ignored by those concerned with policy problems. For them, the world is seen in a perspective that reduces things to a means–end schema: What do we do in order to achieve what we want? This is social science as the handmaiden of policy.

The second source of problems for social science is in the philosophy of history, or more broadly social philosophy. Here we find intellectual problems of great scope, many as old as the history of human thought. In the most general terms, new elements, unknown in their implications, must be fitted into the given context of the culture, reconciled with the known. Such problems grow out of the effort to integrate, in one map of the world, newly discovered regions and continents of knowledge and/or belief.

Such problems originate in the conflict between an ideology, a *weltanschaaung,* and new experiences. What was the meaning of Copernican cosmology for the Judeo-Christian world view? What was the meaning of the newly discovered "savages" of the western hemisphere for urban European man? Later, what was the meaning of Marx's historical determinism for liberal capitalist societies? Such questions are broad and ultimately beyond the grasp of social science, yet they stimulate social inquiry. The concern with primitive societies led to anthropology, the comparative science of societies; concern with Marxism led scholars to compare seriously the different social classes in their relations with the larger society. In short, the questions generated by philosophers and intellectuals, generalists and dilettantes, are fertile sources for social inquiry. (And too, some social scientists have been intellectuals, and some philosophers.)

The aim of such inquiry is, finally, a recreation of intellectual order, an integrated world view. The new knowledge and belief interacts with the older frame of reference; both are changed in the process and much is rejected. The intellectual map of the world is left different. Today no serious thinker concerned with society could ignore the relationship between the organization of economic production and reward and the political (and ideological) life of a society. Nor could he ignore the results of comparative anthropology, which turned the "noble savage" and "the war of each against all" into myths, but in the process greatly broadened our knowledge of the possible forms human life may take.

The focus of such inquiry is, then, upon ways of integrating new phenomena, new ideas, with an older frame of reference. It is an operation in which we abstract from the welter of history and the array of social forms what appear to be massive tendencies, radical innovations in thought and act, as well as the assumed nature of the world before these occurred. In this kind of inquiry there is a tendency toward a conservative bias, for the pre-existing situation is taken as causal and the novel ideas and facts are seen as deriving from it. If, however, the abstract picture of the earlier situation is incorrect (as it often is), the definition of the new may be grossly deformed. Those who interpret the Soviet regime in Russia as a continuation of Tsarist absolutism may purchase a grain of truth at the price of a carload of illusion. (Indeed, one might understand more about Tsarism through studying the Soviets—the data are nearer at hand.)

The third origin of problems in the social sciences is in the emerging questions raised by previously accumulated propositions. These are questions intrinsic to the discipline; they may have significance for policy or social philosophy, but that is not their significance for the scientist. The plotting of "learning curves" may be useful to the teacher, but the research psychologist is concerned with the general theory of learning. Such problems, requiring previously formalized theories, come later in the development of a science than policy problems (which may reflect the vocabulary of the folk culture and the assumptions of causation prevalent in everyday life) or problems of social philosophy (which may rest upon unsystematic and unproven beliefs about history and the nature of society).

Thus the scientific problems are generic to an existing scientific community, or "discipline." They emerge from conflicts between existing theories, conflicts between theories and findings, hiatuses within the theoretical house, and gaps in empirical proof for accepted propositions. Their resolution must either increase the pragmatic scope of the propositions embodied in the science, its "empirical bite," or increase the unity and power of propositions through expanding their theoretical significance. (It is, of course, an achievement to demonstrate that propositions do not have the relevance to the experienced world they are believed to have, for the elimination of error is a necessary condition for truth.)

The solution to a problem of this sort requires focusing upon theory, evidence, and the rules by which each enters into the argument. Thus the scientist working at problems generic to his discipline tries to extend the theoretical structure in the light of new data which he has created through observation, and he tries to extend the meaning of the empirical known by new theory which he has created to accommodate the facts. Such problem-solving may result in rigorous, controlled tests: at an extreme, the "crucial experiment" in which opposing interpretations allow one to focus observation on a given situation in which one or the other must be falsified.

One such crucial experiment was that in which Sherif demonstrated the power of repetition to create norms, or regularities in definitions of situations. Using the "autokinetic phenomenon," exposing subjects in a dark room to an unmoving point of light that appears to move, he found that individuals in isolation will develop strongly patterned but individually varying definitions of how the (unmoving) light moves; and that when individuals can communicate about the phenomenon, they develop strong group patterns—consensus concerning the distance the (still unmoving) light moves. By eliminating the "objective facts" he could demonstrate the tendency of the individual to stabilize phenomena in patterns, and the tendency of groups to organize individual interpretations in patterns. The alternative hypothesis of random projection was clearly disproved.

Such research has only the most indirect relevance for policy problems. Its relevance to the problems of social philosophy requires considerable added information and interpretation. But for the discipline of social psychology, it may fairly be called a "crucial experiment." In the process of generalizing and interpreting the findings for other kinds of individual and group situations, however, its empirical limits emerge: at that point, conflicting evidence leads to conflicting theory and a new "crucial experiment" is possible.

The crucial experiment is relatively rare in social inquiry. More common is the pilot inquiry, the descriptive study, the application of some theory to new data, the collection of new evidence for new hypotheses developed from older notions.

In each case the problem-solver, the scientist, is abstracting from the complexity of experience (including speculation) and formulating a problem that may be irrelevant to both policy and philosophy of history. For this reason, those who are not aware of his disciplinary tradition and the sometimes long and torturous lines of intellectual descent may condemn his work as trivial. And studying how far people think an unmoving light moves can easily sound like a trick or a trivial hobby; but we must remember that a monk studying the blossoms of sweet peas contributed a great deal to our knowledge of genetics. The danger is that of misplacing the grounds for significance. Problems that seem wholly internal to a social science may, in the long run, be of most significance for both policy and philosophy; their solutions may revolutionize our general conceptions of the constraints and possibilities of human action.

RELATIONSHIPS AMONG TYPES OF PROBLEMS IN THE ONGOING ENTERPRISE

We have emphasized that each type of problem that gives rise to social inquiry is an abstraction from the complexity of events. This means that they are not mutually exclusive; policy problems, philosophical problems, and generic scientific problems may coexist in the same research project and indeed in the same social scientist's concerns. This is fortunate, because most social research is supported for its policy implications, and basic scientific inquiry is frequently forced to ride "piggyback."

A case in point is the large-scale research enterprise known as the Metropolitan St. Louis Survey. Financed by tax-exempt foundations, it had as its goal the description of the complex structure of local government in one of our largest metropolitan areas, its evaluation, and recommendations for the improvement of that government. For the policy-oriented, the latter was by far the most important goal; it was the rationale for the investment of a third of a million dollars and thousands of man hours over a year's time.

The research included a careful study of the governmental jurisdictions and structures among the 97 municipalities, several counties, and multitudinous "special district governments" of the metropolis. In order to relate government to needs and resources, the population of the area was also analyzed, which indicated the kinds of neighborhoods enjoying (or not enjoying) the different units of government. And to discover the citizens' evaluations of government and participation in politics, a sample scattered over the entire metropolitan area was intensively interviewed. On the basis of this and other evidence, the Survey staff published description, analysis, and recommendations for change. This information was later used to formulate a new plan of government for the area, which was submitted to the citizens in a referendum.

Some of the social scientists on the Survey staff had interests beyond the improvement of government for metropolitan St. Louis. They were concerned with the loose structure of propositions about "mass society" and contemporary cities popular in contemporary social philosophy. This is the argument that with urbanization, the development of Spengler's massive Cities of the Autumn, the individual becomes lost, isolated from friends, kin, neighbors and community. As he becomes isolated, so the argument runs, he becomes alienated from public affairs and politics, and the local political community atrophies as social fact. "The time of the Caesars" has arrived. Here was an opportunity to explore these propositions with relevant data.

The key concept was *differentiation*. The neighborhoods of a metropolis vary immensely in their social characteristics, and it seemed unlikely that all citizens would be equally isolated and alienated from public affairs. So the analysis of the population by neighborhood (or census tract), already useful to indicate the differences between citizens of the various government units, became a tool for identifying differences in the urban worlds in which the sample survey respondents lived. These varied widely by socioeconomic status, by ethnic background, and importantly, by style of life. By the latter is meant, at one extreme, neighborhoods approaching Wirth's "urbanism as a way of life," in which most people live in apartment houses, many are unmarried, and of those who are few have children and many women work outside the home; at the other extreme are horizontal neighborhoods of single-family "homes" where marriage is the norm, children are rife, and the wife stays home to raise children. The major hypothesis was that the more his neighborhood resembled the latter, the more likely the person interviewed was to be involved in the society and active in its political process.

When the answers to the sample survey questions were analyzed this hypothesis turned out to be accurate. In the most urban neighborhoods people were very often without ties to neighbors or the local community, and they were often uninvolved and incompetent in local public affairs; in the family-centered suburbs the opposite was true. But in neither case was the situation uniform. The vast generalizations of the "mass society hypothesis," couched in terms of either/or, was shifted to propositions about more-than/less-than, and the conditions under which each occurred.

Certain problems generic to the disciplines of sociology, social psychology, and political science were also explored in depth with materials gathered to solve the policy problem. The associational patterns of urbanites were explored in detail, with results challenging certain pre-existing beliefs and qualifying others; the associations of urban Negroes were analyzed and compared with those of whites at the same level of social class; Durkheim's propositions concerning *anomie* were tested; "participational types" were discovered illuminating some of the enormous variations in political competence and involvement among metropolitan citizens.

Thus the Metropolitan St. Louis Survey, primarily designed to improve metropolitan government, allowed inquiry into problems derived from both social philosophy and basic theory in a number of fields. The reform movement, of which it was part, failed resoundingly at the polls. (Which led to a further study of the voting, informed by the knowledge ac-

quired in the earlier study.) The results of the various analyses, however, were the basis for further research in a dozen
other cities in the United States and abroad—just as this
St. Louis research rested upon previous studies in Los Angeles, San Francisco, Chicago, and other cities.

And indeed most fields of concentration for social inquiry
are first defined as policy problems. They grow out of conflict
in the society and are interpreted in the folk language of that
society. Thus the programs to "Americanize the Immigrant,"
and to do something about the "Negro Problem," in early
twentieth-century America led to the intense and cumulative
study of ethnic differentiation and its implications for social
organization. In a similar way, popular shock at crime, prosti-
tution, narcotics addiction, and other "social pathologies" led
eventually to the rigorous study of deviation and control, of
how and why individuals violate the pattern of their society,
and of the social efforts to repair these snags in the fabric.

One may postulate a natural history of social science spe-
cialities. Out of interest couched in the folk frame of reference
develops a public problem; defined as capable of solution, it
becomes a policy problem. Then, as systematic inquiry is
stimulated, it is subjected to the control of the research
cycle, moving toward the status of an intrinsically scientific
problem. The same is true of problems generated by social
philosophy. While, as Merton has suggested, American social
scientists have been more stimulated by policy problems and
European scholars by those derived from the philosophy of
history, both kinds lead to the same end: the basic research
problem, the search for structure and changes in structure,
whose results have caught the attention of practical men or
philosophers, leading them to identify "problems."

In the beginning social inquiry is subsidized by the interests
of the existing community as it defines them. As it develops a
body of empirically grounded propositions having a theoretical
cohesion, it becomes an autonomous and valued enterprise.
The significance generated *within the discipline* becomes a
major criterion for new research. But the state of social inquiry today, somewhere between lore and primitive science,

means that a great deal of our inquiry is couched in terms of common sense, stimulated by concern with policy, rewarded as efforts to contribute to community problem-solving. As a given discipline or specialty within it develops, however, major contributions to basic scientific knowledge are recognized as the greatest achievements of all.

[2]

THE ASSUMPTIONS OF
SOCIAL SCIENCE

A favorite shibboleth concerning the social scientist when he applies his knowledge to a policy problem is that "he has no preconceived notions." The facts, the given, will be the basis for his judgment. But in truth all of us must bring such notions to any bit of the world that catches our attention; we assign millions of significances in our everyday life.

Indeed, it requires a strenuous act of control to view any scene without meanings from our past. Yet if one is completely empirical what is given is experience *minus* these meanings. We try to eliminate all previous assumptions until we are left with the primitive, the knower's field of consciousness. This has been described as a point of awareness in an esthetic continuum, a field differentiated by tones, colors, sensations of the various organs. In such a rigorous abstraction, the classroom is only a blur of nameless colors, sounds, and scents. It requires an enormous number of assumptions to assign meanings even to physical objects: this chair is merely a colored shape, an impression on buttocks and back, until we call upon our accumulated beliefs. And, much more complex, these students are puzzles without some theory of society and the process of socialization. In short, the "immediately apprehended" world is utterly without meaning.

This primitive way of approaching the world, shorn of preconceptions, is the most empirical approach possible. It relies upon no theory, no intellectual construct. It is the way of the mystic who "empties his mind" and makes no distinction between subject and object, the self and what it experiences. So far from the everyday experience of mankind is a really radical and pure empiricism that only exotics—practitioners of yoga, introspective philosophy, "action" painting, and psychophysical research—use it.

Even in this experience, however, one may question what is known. One knows the world only through his own specific windows—is it not possible that he knows *only* the windows? Remember the Chinese poet who dreamed he was a bluebottle fly, and on waking did not know if he was a poet remembering a dream or a bluebottle fly dreaming he was a poet. Our distinction between dream and waking must certainly be based upon more than immediate sensation. But if one is a radical empiricist, that is all he has to work with.

Such considerations open the way for a purely solipsistic position. Here the only reality, the only thing one can know, is the self, a knowledge that cannot be available to anyone else. But, by the same token, it is *the* truth—and can never be communicated. The argument is simple: All I can know is that which is immediately available to me, therefore what I know is true because *I* know it (the ultimate criterion of a primitive empiricism).

The position is logically unassailable. However, when a person holding it adduces *any* data not immediately given he is betraying his argument. And in social interaction it is impossible to avoid such assumptions; one assumes a world and its habits, a language and its structure, for only a language held in common allows us to develop and defend the solipsistic position. But the moment one makes such assumptions he is betraying his argument by his actions. The very nature of human life falsifies his major assumptions: what then is implied?

Having suspended belief (or emptied our mind) we then must choose new belief in order to say anything at all. But now the assumptions may in principle be freely chosen elements, not givens of our culture and our past learning. These assumptions cannot, ultimately, be proven, for they are the beginning in terms of which any proof is possible. If I do not assume that some things cause other things you cannot prove it to me; if you do not assume the existence of a supreme deity I cannot prove its existence to you without relying upon it as given. But to do so is to assume one's own conclusions (as with those believers who prove the existence of God or dialectical materialism through quoting the Bible or Marx). This is, needless to say, an ineffective method of persuasion.

The scientific mode of processing experience rests upon a triad of major assumptions. First, one must assume the existence of a world beyond the senses. It is a world which conditions them and is not wholly controlled by them. This assumption is necessary if we are to avoid the solipsistic circle in which nothing is true save that which is unavailable to others. Second, we must assume that this world is knowable by humanity through some process, and that a process which allows communication. Third, we must assume the value of knowing the results of interaction with that world, and thus the value of accumulating knowledge of it.

None of these three assumptions is self-evident. None can be proved without assuming one's own conclusions. One must then ask the naïve question: Why do we choose to make them?

There are, at least, pragmatic reasons. We make the major assumptions underlying science because we believe they will pay off in terms of our goals—whatever they are. The test of the assumptions lies, then, in the use to which we put them, the structure of meaning that can be erected on this foundation and its value to us in our ongoing concerns. At the crudest level technology, tools for the manipulation of the world, is a kind of proof.

But one may have technology without science and one may reject technologies and still accept the basic assumptions underlying science. Indeed, one can conceive of a society with a simple technology and a very complex science (we might all be safer under such a regime). A second, more subtle and for me more compelling reason to accept the major assumptions lies in their esthetic possibilities. We may choose these assumptions as materials, from which to create a more powerful and consistent view of human experience. Bases for a possible order, they are validated by the clarity and unity that the developing sciences contribute to our grasp of the larger human situation.

Such assumptions as underlie science, once made, amount to serious commitments. They are coercive in ways easily overlooked, for we gloss them over with use and assume them to be given in the nature of things. Their coerciveness is manifest in our own thought: all future argument finally depends upon one's basic assumptions for final validity. At the same time, the coerciveness of scientific discourse stems from the root assumptions. If all parties to an argument hold these same assumptions, it then becomes possible to force agreement through the use of logical analysis. (For logic is simply a way of spelling out all that is implicit in the original commitments.)

The coerciveness of assumptions, however, is also revealed in our inability to argue to a conclusion with those holding different positions. One can argue with a mystic only if he accepts the distinction between an "inner world" and "outer conditions." If he holds that true reality is a unity known only in given states of being, neither Freudian theory nor behaviorist psychology offers any ground for discussion with him. His assumptions differ too radically. So also with the thoroughgoing Marxist. You can argue politics and economics with him only if he sees them as problems of knowledge; if he says I believe this because it is inherent in my nature because of my position in society at this point in history you have no grounds whatsoever for argument. Both the Yogi and the Commissar are outside the scientific realm of discourse.

There is a final and grim implication. If men do not share basic assumptions there is no way to reach agreement. They must either coexist symbiotically, without basic argument, or when they reach ineluctable conflict, forego persuasion. If I assume God or the Dialectic and you do not we can never reach agreement. Our only recourse will be to mount a crusade. And in the words of Kenneth Rexroth: "History is the record of Man's mostly unsuccessful efforts to find a significant ground for conflict." In short, when discourse fails war takes over. The argument goes to the biggest battalions.

THE ASSUMPTIONS NECESSARY
FOR SOCIAL SCIENCE

Translating these assumptions of science we can state three major beliefs underlying the social sciences. First, there is a social world that conditions us and is not completely controllable by us. Second, it is a knowable world, a social fact. Finally, it is worth our while to know that world. None of these is self-evident; all are chosen options.

Randall Jarrell has described some grimmer aspects of the social world in "The Death of the Ball-Turret Gunner":

> From my mother's sleep I fell into the State,
> And I hunched in her belly till my wet fur froze;
> Six miles from earth, loosed from its dream of life
> I woke to black flak and the nightmare fighters.
> When I died they washed me out of
>   the turret with a hose.

The ball-turret gunner sat in a bubble of glass under the belly of the giant flying fortresses of World War II. If the glass were broken at a high altitude his death was instant and messy.

More interesting than this vulnerability of physical structure, however, is another kind that illuminates the power of social structure. The ball-turret gunner had a special place in the bomber crew; a certain pathos surrounded anyone who had this job. The entire assembly in which he sat could be withdrawn into the belly of the plane, but the machinery for this made it very heavy; the cost was decreased flying speed. For this reason it was so constructed that the hydraulic machinery for raising and lowering the turret, together with the turret and the gunner, could all be detached and dropped off the plane. Further, the bomber crew was trained so that in the event of close pursuit, when greater speed was necessary to save the plane and crew, the captain's orders were to drop the ball-turret, gunner and all, through the six miles to earth. Now a bomber crew tended to develop strong *esprit de corps,* affection and mutual respect. Yet here was a sacrificial animal, one who was both a comrade and a physical obstacle to escape; thus the pathos of the role.

The social structure producing the situation of the ~~gunner~~ *patient* was outside the control of any given captain or gunner; indeed, their lives were ordered to a program none had made. Thus an outsider can look at that order and understand its imperatives and its rigidity, knowing nothing of the individuals who comprise it. The order, a set of relationships among the component parts of the crew, is as solid as a wall of brick. And indeed the structure of social action is sometimes literally a "wall," as in the solid wall of angry whites barring Negro children from school in a Southern town, or the phalanx of bodies in military close-order drill.

Social science has been called the study specializing in "the architecture of the maze," while psychology is the study of the rats' behavior in it. The paradoxical aspect of this lies in the circumstance that we are each, simultaneously, both the rat running the maze and one face in the wall of faces that defines the architecture of the thing. As we are constrained by the patterned behavior of others, so our own ordered behavior creates the limits within which they must act.

One well-known discussion of the matter is Durkheim's. In his view, social science is the study of "social fact" and only social fact. This fact is characterized by externality and constraint. He believed that much of our behavior can be explained only by the external social world, whose giant regularities and trends of change carry the given individual along without respect to his wishes, constraining his behavior and allowing the possibility of scientific explanation through a knowledge of that systematic constraint. Thus he chose suicide, "the most private behavior," as a test; he demonstrated that the incidence of this most private behavior varied predictably with the state of the total society in which the individual lived and from which he departed. In the same fashion, "individualism" as a creed is a product of a society whose folk thought stresses it. We are all in large measure conformists, and for a very good reason; any society requires predictable behavior, achieved through rules to which most people conform most of the time.

But a qualification is in order. Social science deals only with that which is social in nature, that is, the mutual modification of behavior. Yet individual human beings include much more activity than that oriented toward and constrained by the patterns of social relationship. The latter is abstracted from the totality (one meaning of abstraction is "to take out"), treated as reality *sui generis,* because it manifests an order apart from the complexity of the total individual. This does not negate the latter; indeed, it can help to clarify it.

Out of the complexity of individual experience comes variation from the existing rules. It may be in the form of error resulting from social and physical accident—the giant among dwarfs, the retarded child. It may also emerge from the ongoing symbolic processes in the individual—fantasy, conscious thought, dreams (Delmore Schwartz's poem title, "In Dreams Begin Responsibilities," is often literally correct), and it may emerge in overt action that cannot be explained, or even confronted, purely on social scientific grounds. Thus we have at one extreme the psychopathic killer; at another, the creative genius. Neither is unaffected by the maze of social constraints; neither can be satisfactorily explained in those terms. The rat is also a system.

There is some human experience that does not fall within the assumptions of science. Not only in dreaming, but in any moment of feeling we are experiencing what can accurately be called the "ineffable." It is incommunicable precisely because of the separateness of identity; here is the strain of truth in the solipsist's position. The closest contact of the most passionate lovers still leaves them separate individuals, finally alone with their experience. It is for these reasons that the ancient epigram is still valid: *de gustibus non disputan-*

dum est. For disputes over taste cannot be settled logically or
empirically, since subjective states cannot be proven to be
identical. Thus a wide range of human experience cannot be
explained by social science, nor can beliefs about it be objectively validated.

And even beyond the esthetics of experience lie other
ranges of phenomena that the scientific assumptions exclude.
These include all that cannot be made accessible to human
sensibility. Lest this sound too simpleminded, let us remember that deity is often conceived in such terms and, for this
reason, is not subject to scientific argument. The communi-
cant of a religion can always say: "Science deals with the
structure of the world, but my god is not interested in that
structure." To be sure, such a position gives enormous ground
to science. It is close to that of Santayana, who spoke of
religion as "the poetry of human aspiration," and contended
that when it extended beyond that it typically produced "bad
physics and false prophecy."

In short, social science is one abstraction out of human experience. Like all abstractions, it does not exhaust the subject;
its incompleteness yields a power not directly relevant to all
human concerns. But it is not in this matter unique among
our ways of knowing the world.

The discussion of assumptions has been rather prolonged
for the reason that awareness of assumptions greatly increases the possibilities for intellectual order. Knowing the
assumptions of science, and social science, also makes it easier
for us to avoid confusion, for the aspects of experience to
which they are appropriate and inappropriate become easier
to identify, and many useless arguments may be avoided.

A clear understanding of assumptions also increases intellectual power and freedom. You can, for one thing, always
return to your root assumptions when the argument becomes
self-contradictory, when the theory does not work. You can
delete or add or modify the assumptions in the light of the
conflict stemming from them.

There are, furthermore, many choice points in creating

valid social science. For some of them there is no empirically or logically given priority of choice. They are matters for each social scientist to work out on his own—choices based on intellectual style and the field of interest as it exists at a given time. We may have powerful personal preferences in these matters; they remain preferences. But if the nature of the choice point can be clearly identified and some consequences flowing from a given choice made clear, then it is easier to choose and to change one's mind if work down the way indicates the choice was inappropriate.

All of us, social scientists and laymen, have to make such choices anyway—though their salience varies with one's interest. Like the bourgeois gentleman who spoke prose without knowing it, we are all methodologists in spite of ourselves. The nature of conscious human life forces it upon us. If so, it seems worthwhile to know what we are buying; we may want to return it to the store.

[3]

SENSE DATA, FRAME OF
REFERENCE, AND FACT

The social scientist is committed to knowing the world beyond his immediate experience. Indeed it is fair to say that he seeks to understand himself through observing the behavior of others. Yet all he is given directly is his own esthetic experience, his perception and his humors (that which we label variously love, grief, anxiety, elation, depression). Somehow the esthetic present must be related to that which is beyond the senses, dark *noumena* relatively free of our subjective control. What is beyond in time and space must be related to the immediate.

One thing is certain; the process of knowing must include two terms. It cannot lie exclusively within the individual consciousness—this is solipsism again and we have already assumed more than that. Yet it cannot be exclusive to the world "out there"; sense impressions do not come to us bearing labels of theoretical significance. They do not generalize; we do. The world out there can only be known as experience is processed through the human intelligence. There are neither chairs nor students nor colleges in nature until we create them.

But we have no inherent gift, no touchstone, for determining the degree to which our creations correspond to the habits of the world. This is clear in Sherif's experiments with the autokinetic phenomenon (chapter 1). It is made dramatically clear in our response to an instrument used in psychological research. Here a revolving electric fan is illuminated by a focused light in an otherwise darkened room. The light is arranged to flash periodically, so that the fan blades are glimpsed only at intervals; by changing the periodicity of the light one can make the fan appear to turn faster, to slow down, to come to a dead stop. The unwary empiricist, trusting to his senses, could easily lose a hand if he tested his belief and thrust it into the "unmoving" blades.

It is indeed a dangerous world, where seeing is not believing. Nor, be it noted, is believing necessarily seeing; both modern psychology and nuclear physics make this clear. Instead, what is seen is a clue to belief, and what is believed a clue to what is seen. In short, intelligence is not an attribute of the individual as an entity; it is a state of the individual's transactions with his environment, what is outside him and around him in time and space. Intelligence is a shorthand word for a pattern that may break down at any moment and truth is a complex relationship among subject, concept, and sense data. The empiricist who stuck his hand into the apparently unmoving fan would be operating with an inadequate concept; the more accurate one would include not only the nature of fans but also the nature of fans in periodically flashing light beams. Frequently we are in his position; the world is full of booby traps (and thus the origin of boobs).

In John James's summary phrase, these considerations indicate "the neutrality of the human nervous system." All truth and all falsehood are equally natural, native to us, and determinable only in the light of other knowledge than that given in the immediate scene. Thus the totalitarian regime, controlling all mass media and news from the outside, can convince most citizens that wars are thrust upon the state by its enemies; without comparative data and subjected only to managed news through many years and millions of words, the argument becomes coercive. McLuhan's thesis, that the media for communication extend and change our sensibility, indicates a truth. Today, as Suzanne Langer puts it: "the edifice of human knowledge stands before us, not as a vast collection of sense reports, but as a structure of *facts that are symbols* and *laws that are their meanings*." This is not because the nature

of human knowledge has changed (though there is that too)
but because our analysis of knowing penetrates deeper into
those mysterious transactions between men and the universe.

So we obviously go far beyond the empirical evidence of
our senses. We project from the immediate situation to other
times and places; we anticipate and predict. And we do this
by perceiving patterns in the world and assuming structures
that underlie those patterns. In short, we process and organize the given sense data.

They are the beginning. They may be conceived as the
contact of a structure with an environment, the relations between the reflective individual and the results of transactions
with noumena beyond the grasp of the senses. Our reactions
are not then identical with the world that provokes them; we
are more like the stranger in a dark house colliding with the
shapes of unfamiliar furniture. The vibration, the thing we
call "light," affects our surfaces and our response is a perception we call "blue," though vibrations are not blue and color
does not often vibrate. Even the concept of blue is not ineluctable; there are societies without names or use for many
shades of color which we consider given.

We are subject to a continual rain of potential stimuli.
Out of these we respond to certain wave lengths, in certain
ways. But our senses are limited in number and in range: certain high-fidelity sound reproduction is audible only by dogs.
We filter the world through our senses and in this rain of
stimuli no causal complexes whatsoever are given.

Yet the sense data are organized. Through repetition of
similar experiences they are transformed into complexes corresponding to some of the habits of the world. Recall becomes
prediction; as we experience part of a complex we expect to
find the wonted whole, in space or time, following upon it
in an orderly fashion. When complexes are important enough
we develop symbols to name them, to summarize them, to
evoke them when they are not present. At the simplest level,
the symbol "hot" refers to certain responses in some kinds of
situations. The responses are memorable; the burnt child
fears the fire.

Symbols stand for concepts, but what then are concepts? We shall discuss them in detail later; for now let us simply say that concepts are *forms* abstracted from complexes of experience. Since they are abstract forms, they can refer to a wide range of experience; that is, they have generality. Thus out of the concept "hot" develops the concept "heat," a complex and many-termed abstraction summarizing a few aspects of experience under a great variety of circumstances—from the hot iron on the foot to the heat of a summer day to estimates of the heat on the surface of the sun.

All discourse demands concepts. For discourse requires that we abstract, out of the whole stream of experience, limited aspects that are interesting and communicable through those symbols we call language. Science, as a variety of discourse, is even more demanding than most discourse. Then the question becomes: How do you abstract? What do you keep and what do you ignore? To be sure, in one sense everything is related to everything and all causes all, but this is unedifying even though correct. We must discriminate—that is, abstract.

There is absolutely no rule for abstraction. All that can be said is that we select our sense data as we believe them to be interesting, pertinent to our purposes, relevant to our frame of reference. Thus a foreman's actions can be viewed by his supervisor as useful or not in the ongoing work of the plant; by his minister as clues to the state of his immortal soul; by a psychologist as a clue to his relations with his father; by a sociologist as indicative of the strains built into a social role halfway between management and the workers. The frame of reference, which highlights our interest and excludes other aspects of an event, determines the sense data to which we attend. Our view of Elysian Park will be very different when we are taking a Sunday stroll than when we are fleeing for our lives.

But there are limits on the concepts useful to the scientist. When a painter was sketching the machinery and men at work in a large industrial plant a worker, looking over his shoulder, protested that the drawing of a machine was inaccurate. "If it were like that it simply wouldn't work!" He was answered:

"It doesn't have to work as a drill-press—it has to work as a piece of art." The picture of the world the social scientist creates must work in both senses: it must have fidelity to the original, the social machine, and it must have clarity and communicability. His frame of reference demands hard facts in working order.

ON THE NATURE OF FACT

The term "fact" is pivotal; all science adduces it sooner or later. Yet it is by no means so simple as common-sense discourse assumes; as we have seen, the facts can never "speak for themselves." Part of the difficulty is our tendency to place facts "out there" in the environment; we can do this, however, only as long as we have already conceptualized that environment. If facts are, in fact, "intellectually formulated events," most of the formulations we use in everyday life are inherited from our cultural ancestors. As we share a culture with others, that culture is the basis for our version of "common sense." Since this is the result of powerful lifelong habits, we tend to ignore the learning aspect and thus confuse the *fact* with the *event* itself.

John Dewey's conception of fact seems most useful. To paraphrase, a fact is a complex of sense data organized with respect to a prior frame of reference. Thus a person's past experience determines what he sees, gives it meaning for him, and on the basis of that meaning he reacts to the intellectual formulation of the event. There are a number of important implications.

For one, it is clear that there are no given facts apart from one's prior definition. The hard fact is that all facts are in part intellectual constructs. This is equally true of geological strata and human neuroses and, as Cooley once remarked, the facts of social life are our expectations of the expectations of others. Concreteness is simply the result of our unquestioning acceptance of the intellectual formulation together with the dependability of its fit with the nature of things; what we expect occurs. When that does not happen, when the moving blade of the fan strikes us, then we re-examine the obviously misfit "facts" we have been creating.

A second major implication of Dewey's conception is that no fact is inclusive of any given event. No description can exhaust empirical reality. For it is in the nature of our frames of reference to select out of the complex of experience those sense data pertinent to our interests of the moment, losing the rest in the undifferentiated background. This is most clear, perhaps, in the case of art: the successive styles of painting produce pictures so various that they seem to come from different worlds—and they do. But in the same way, the approach of sociologist, economist, or psychologist to the same historical event may result in radically different views of the social world. Such variation tells us nothing about the validity of a given approach; it simply indicates that facts are as various as frames of reference, the human experience a rich and inexhaustible mine of them.

It is also clear that any fact is at the mercy of the frame of reference that allows us to select it. That frame of reference may be useless, may be scientifically dead. In such case the facts collected have no value, though they are clear hard facts. We might remember the false science of phrenology, which purported to study human personality through inspecting the shape of the individual cranium; the result was an impressive collection of fact about bumps and curves on the human head, but nothing useful about personality. More important in the history of science, but equally futile in its results, was Cesare Lombroso's attempt to explain criminality by isolating "criminal types," people who just looked like evil-doers. Varieties of physiognomy were discovered—hard, useless fact.

Finally, it should always be remembered that the frame of reference is pre-existent to the facts it allows us to create. Logically and psychologically prior to the fact, it limits, defines, and in this sense *determines* the facts that one can see. This is dramatically evident in language systems; we typically use one word for snow, not bothering to differentiate much, while the Eskimo have thirty words for the white, light stuff. So important is snow to them, as environment, resource, and threat, that their frame of reference places great emphasis on its kind and amount. We, on the other hand, make distinctions concerning law and justice incomprehensible to the members of their stateless society.

But if our fact is created by our frame of reference, and that in turn derives from our group learning, our culture, where did the scientific frame come from? It is clearly not an inescapable one, for many societies never developed sciences. Yet we cannot have scientific fact until we have a scientific framework for abstracting, out of all we can experience, that which is scientifically useful.

The case seems to be that science, beginning with "fact," really begins with a folk frame of reference. Out of the facts identified by the culture, the common-sense scheme of things, emerge problems of relationship that are scientifically interesting. It has been said that the man who threw the first stone invented the science of mechanics, the one who discovered fire the science of chemistry. The germ of truth in this is that these discoveries made possible certain classes of fact that eventually became building blocks for intellectual problem-solving and abstract theory. It is likely, then, that technology usually precedes the development of science; only as a science matures does its value for technology become apparent.

We have already noted one example of such primitive technology, in Lombroso's classification of criminals. All societies produce criminals if they have laws to define them, and crime is a problem by folk definition. As societies increase in scale and complexity the problem, in parallel fashion, does likewise; in urban societies with the possibilities for anonymity and escape and the rich opportunities available, crime is defined as a major social problem, thus a policy matter. Its cause and cure become matters of public import, and people struggle to understand in order to prevent and cure such behavior.

This kind of problem, the problem of everyday life, yields

a folk definition, one that equates criminal behavior with moral evil. Thus crime is located in the nature of the individual, and sure enough early criminology was focused upon the study of mental traits of criminals. Many studies were carried out contrasting convicted persons with the general population. Unfortunately for this folk theory, confusing and contradictory evidence on the mental traits of criminals emerged. Indeed, one summary study indicated that convicted criminals sometimes appeared more intelligent and emotionally better adjusted on the average than the average law-abiding citizen —and then we remember that these were captive criminals, apt to be less intelligent than the successful who elude the law. Folk thought did not carry us far in solving this problem.

Edwin Sutherland approached the same phenomena and, in the light of such findings, questioned the importance of individual traits. Instead, he located crime in the context of social learning, as one more culture complex learned from others. The usual criminal was the person who had the opportunity to learn the skills of burglary, the confidence game, pocket-picking and the like, and the opportunity to practice them. Thus one looked for those who associated most with criminals, in neighborhood, gang, or employment, to be more likely to commit criminal acts themselves. Further, one looked at *differential association*—how much and how salient was a man's social participation in criminal groups as compared with participation in groups of noncriminals?

This is not the place to discuss this interesting line of inquiry in detail. The important thing to note is that Sutherland, emphasizing social learning, looked at facts entirely different from those mental traits which had preoccupied early social scientists. They had taken folk thought about crime (much of which is still popular) and had exercised more control over their observations, using standard tests and control groups; they had required more of their theory in the way of prediction, and the theory had failed. Then Sutherland turned from individual fact to social fact; not individual traits, but rates of differential association were the facts he required.

But the theory of differential association has much wider applicability. The theory of the "subculture," the norms and beliefs current among one isolated group that make it different from others in the surrounding society, rests upon similar assumptions. Whether one studies "hipsters," the "black gang" on a steamship, the life of the jazz musician, or the persistence of ethnic patterns long after a group has adjusted to a new environment, the general theory of differential association is useful. The problem of everyday life, couched in folk terms, gives rise to a new frame of reference, which has much broader utility than in the problem which stimulated its development.

[4]

SYMBOLIZATION AND MEANING

It is clear that the environment of humanity is symbolically formed and ordered. The brute impression of stimuli has no meaning; the bare facts are far from bare. Formulated events, facts, are symbols of significance to the human actor. What then are we to make of this process by which we create symbols basic to reality?

One influential view has been that of the evolutionary school. Man is seen as the most complex primate and his symbolic processes as a more highly developed form of that which is found in the lower animals. This argument is based upon studies of animals, of children, and of preliterate societies. (Though generalizing from the latter loses popularity, as it becomes clear that even the most primitive society is very complex indeed.) The basic tenet is: symbolization is an adaptive response to given needs in relation to the environment. The result is survival of the individual and, through the individual, the species.

According to this view, symbolization has its roots in the conditioned response. Like Pavlov's dogs, human beings respond to symbols as signs of things not perceived but likely, on the basis of past experience, to be present in some definable relationship. Thus psychology is reduced to biology, albeit of a complex sort; we can hold to the dictum "nothing in man not present in the amoeba." This simple mechanistic approach has found particular favor with the Soviets, as it consorted well with their deterministic theory of human behavior; indeed, Pavlovian behaviorism was a major basis for the Russian educational system after the Revolution. Education is, in this

37

view, a form of conditioning. (We often make this assumption unconsciously; it is implicit in our substitution of "training" for "education.")

There is, however, one major difference between man and the laboratory animals. Whereas they take the ringing bell as evidence of the proximity of food and salivate accordingly, man uses his cues to refer to things past and future and even to things nonexistent. He uses signals to represent as well as to indicate. While the dogs can wag their tails at the indication of hamburger, men can discuss the price of hamburger in relation to its quality, its origins, and the question of whether hamburger should ever have been invented. Thus there is more to account for than the conditioned response to a sign.

But this is explained as a further development of the conditioned response. Language is a more complex sign used to evoke commonly experienced situations and objects, present or not. Out of the social organization of men (one of their important survival tools) developed the necessity to communicate about past and future and distant events; the use of symbolism allowed cooperation and mutual aid. Pointing to situations not present, words allowed the evocation of common past experience as well as anticipation of the future.

Further, the extension from vocal pointing and howling of approval or disapproval in the present to the verbal evocation of many scenes allowed for a greatly complicated thought process. For thought, in this view, is simply suppressed speech: thought begins with the dialogue, but if one is in a situation where he cannot speak aloud, he speaks to a hypostasized "other"—that is, he thinks. There have been intriguing experiments that support this contention; for example, when deaf-mutes are given problems to solve individually, their hands grow tense and move involuntarily, indication of an impulse to communicate with others, rather than simply to think through the problems. Thus from conditioned reflex to vocal expression to verbal expression to thought, the chain of causation is plausible, simple, and satisfying.

George Herbert Mead, the social psychologist, carries the argument further. Using the metaphor of the game, he discusses the way we are actually formed as social persons through our interaction with others, our role contingent upon theirs and theirs upon ours. We relate to them, therefore, through anticipating their future behavior; but this relating is dependent on what they anticipate of us. The individual self is built around a strong armature of social fact: what others expect of us becomes the basis for what we expect of ourselves. Our very self-image is a result of "taking the standpoint of the other" to view our own person and behavior, and the origin of conscience is social, that most solitary voice a precipitate of games we play with groups.

In this view the group precedes the individual, the social precedes the psychological. A number of scholars have followed this lead in studying the emergence of a "self concept" in the child through studying his language. In referring to himself the child progresses from the use of his first name (or "Baby") to "me" to, finally, "I." As he becomes less dependent he ceases to regard himself as object, after his parents, and becomes subject—"I." In the beginning, so it is assumed, his assumption of identity is a by-product of his efforts to adapt to the demands of his nurturing parents and to increase his control over his environment through anticipating their behavior and manipulating it. Then the "I" becomes an integrative symbol which increases his power to control, while the "me" stands for the social order, what he must conform to and, more important, what he uses to evaluate his own behavior.

In this view then, symbolization is merely the "latest extension of practical intelligence," to use Suzanne Langer's words. It is adaptive behavior that increases our individual probability of maximizing reward and minimizing punishment through conforming to the group's symbol system. For the group, it maximizes the chance of survival through facilitating cooperation and the resulting control of the environment, thus maintaining man's ecological niche, his place in the biological scheme of things.

This set of arguments, persuasive as it is, has been challenged by Langer. Noting the importance to human life of

ritual, art, and dream, she points out how very disadvanta-
geous they may be to the survival of group or individual. We
know of societies whose ritual requirements for boat-building
became so complex and demanding that they were unable to
build a boat; others have so elaborated their taboos on mate
selection that a "ritual crime" is necessary even to perpetuate
the breed. As for art, only a fool would commit himself to the
fine arts in the United States as a way of gaining food, cloth-
ing, and shelter; many thousands of fools do so. (There are
approximately 20,000 easel painters in New York City alone,
according to the 1960 census.) And as for dream—it is a
complex and wasteful activity. These may be regarded as
"pathologies" of symbolization, yet if they are, why do they
persist and even increase in importance? Maladaptations are
not supposed to have such survival value. War apparently
will survive to the end, even though this kind of ritual is
proven deadly to the species. There is more to life than adaptation.

Langer develops an alternative:

"I propose, therefore, to try a new general principle: to conceive
the mind, still as an organ in the service of primary needs, but of
characteristically human needs; instead of assuming that the human
mind tries to do the same thing as a cat's mind, but by the use of a
special talent which miscarries four times out of five, I shall assume
that the human mind is *trying to do something else;* and that the
cat does not act humanly because he *does not need to.* This difference in fundamental needs, I believe, determines the difference of
function which sets man so far apart from all his zoological breth-
ren . . . .

The basic need, which certainly is obvious only in man, is the
need of symbolization. The symbol-making function is one of man's
primary activities, like eating, looking, or moving about. It is the
fundamental process of his mind, and goes on all the time. Sometimes we are aware of it, sometimes we merely find its results, and
realize that certain experiences have passed through our brains
and have been digested there."

It is a view of human experience that postulates a symbolic metabolism corresponding to our physical metabolism.

Sense experience is interpreted, transformed, stored, and it emerges in various forms of gesture and verbal behavior. It may be at the level of symbolic babbling, but it can result in conversation, gossip, and eventually the novel (that art form developed from gossip). Versions of experience are created, shared, exchanged. Jokes are made, clowns are created in the gang, and the dead are kept with us in memory. The assumption of the "something other" in man seems necessary.

Symbolization is not thought. It occurs prior to thought and creates essential materials for that complex activity. Out of recall, imagination, and sense data emerge our symbols. From such experience we develop our "personal knowledge," our primitive ideas. Then through social discourse, through making them understandable to others, we isolate what is communicable about them—consciously or no, we conceptualize.

"Because," says Langer, "our brain is only a fairly good transmitter, but a tremendously powerful transformer, we do things that (any) cat would reject as too impractical, if he were able to conceive them. So they would be, for him; so are they for the psychologist who deems himself a cat of the nth degree." And out of this symbolic transformation come dreams, art, ritual—and those elements of everyday life that are dreamlike, esthetic and ritualistic. The primitive esthetic component in all experience, made inescapable by the nature of our senses, is greatly magnified by our creation of symbols.

To be sure, efforts have been made to explain the esthetic and symbolific through its utility for individual or group. An entire (divided) school of thought called "functionalism" rests upon such assumptions. Thus Durkheim speaks of ritual as useful in maintaining group solidarity, especially in the presence of threat. But explanation through final results is dangerous indeed: it is doubtful if the ritual found universally among preliterate people resulted from social engineering on the part of the group. In this kind of approach the danger is that of saying: "Fish have fins in order to swim." More useful and to the point is the simpler statement: "Fish, having fins, are able to swim."

Langer's position is preferable because, paradoxically, it

assumes less than does the evolutionary approach. The valued
relationship with the environment (social and otherwise),
celebrated through ritual, precedes and supports the social
consequences of ritual. Having ritual, it is then possible for
us to experience solidarity: in the long run groups without
ritual may suffer (Langer argues this is true of the United
States today), and those with ritual may fare better in the
world. But underlying that ritually achieved solidarity, again,
is man's tendency to symbolize, which often makes him appear
mad in his waking life, but which may save him from madness
when he dreams and, dreaming, reintegrates the jumbled
parts of his symbolic world.

SYMBOLS AND THE NATURE
OF MEANING

Symbols are items of a communication process. That process
may go on *within* the individual only, or *between* individuals.
The symbols are created by man's peculiar view of the world,
his "abstractive seeing," and are retained in memory and
habits. They have both logical and psychological meanings—
logical in their public order, psychological in the individual's
response to and use of them.

Their psychological meaning inheres in the individual
memory. Symbols store past experiences and evoke them in
the form of conceptions of the world, then or now. They allow us to relate many varieties of remembered experience,
through the use of analogy (when we note similarity of forms)
and through association within a larger whole, or *gestalt*. Thus
by analogy we note the similarity of the digital computer to
the human mind: both store, process, and describe the data
fed in. (The computer is more accurate, the mind more interesting.) We associate within a larger whole when the smell
of fire evokes fear based on past experience of pain. For concepts need not be visual or verbal; all of the senses are con-
ceptually creative as they select and exclude.

The natural history of psychological meaning is from sense

data to symbol to the individual's system of meaning to the resulting interpretation of the experience. This interpretation emerges from past experience, and sets the experience within a larger context or, as we sometimes say, places it at a "more general level." Thus, for example, we may examine two marks on a stone and conceive one mark as a six-pointed star, a Star of David, the other as a crudely smeared "hooked cross," or swastika, the stone as a grave marker. This conception, in turn, can evoke the whole bitter history of the Jews in Nazi Germany, which can then be considered in the framework of ethnic differences among men or in the framework of a theory of persecution, from the witch trials in Salem to the camp at Auschwitz.

The logical aspect of symbols inheres in social communication among actors sharing a given conceptual vocabulary. It refers, not to the individual conceptions evoked by the symbol, but to those *concepts* that are sharable and mean approximately the same to all who speak the language. In Langer's terms, "That which all adequate conceptions of an object must have in common, is the concept of the object." But we must ask, adequate to what?

Concepts must be adequate to the individual conceptions evoked, for one thing. For another, they must be adequate to evoke conceptions having a basic, formal similarity among individuals, allowing communication; this is sometimes referred to as intersubjective reliability. Thus it is clear that concepts are more "abstract" than individual conceptions; in concepts the richness and variety of evocations not essential to the form are secondary. The concept results from the (usually unconscious) selection in discourse of those aspects of conceptions held in common. They are simpler, "flatter," than all that is evoked by the symbol in any given individual; they hold their form through their *definition* (delimitation) by the group, whether by the memory of the old men of the tribe or through Dr. Johnson's dictionary. Concepts are similar to platitudes in speech, stereotypes in social relations. Much is left out, but the result is an increase in ease and clarity of communication.

With self-consciousness in discourse a language becomes more ordered, terms become more delimited. Rules are developed for avoiding and undoing confusion; consistency of usage becomes important. Logic, made conscious as a tool of argument, allows an argument to reach resolution: a man may be forced to admit he is in error, or confess he is inconsistent (i.e., a fool). But logic in its specialized sense, as a developed skill, is rare; most societies have only a folk logic, with rules only for those decisions considered important in the view of the members.

Thus the judicial logic of the Anglo-Saxon traditions is quite irrelevant to judgment among some peoples. Paul Bohannon reports that among the Nigerian society called the Tiv the aim in a trial is not to find the facts and mete out justice in terms of precedent and principle, but to restore a state of equable relations among *all* the parties to a quarrel. In the process, judicial logic as we know it goes by the board, but the Tiv with his folk logic would be amazed at American law ways.

Logic is a discipline for clarifying discourse. With increasing complexity a society generates more situations requiring clarity; in groups as various as practitioners in the legal profession, the church, the military, the university, and the scientific laboratory, the strict use of terms and logical "operations" becomes valued. Formal logic, from Aristotle to Wittgenstein, sets new standards for concepts. The public nature of language, always implicitly there, is explicitly noted and linguistic structure becomes an area for intensive inquiry.

Figure 4.1 diagrams the discussion thus far. The sense data on the gravestone, in its symbolic aspects, led to the conception of Nazism and Jewry which defined the meaning of the object to the subject. The line of impact between conception and subject is what is usually called connotation, that between object and subject, denotation. In discourse the latter is usually simply assumed, for the concept represents it in memory. Thus if one were recounting the experience to a friend, the verbal symbols would evoke through concepts the implied objects gravestone, swastika, and star, to be fleshed, however, with another esthetic imagination.

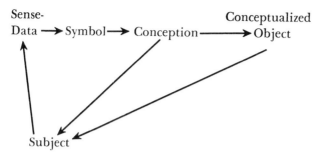

FIGURE 4.1. Symbolization

In contrast to the process of symbolization, let us diagram the nature of signification, the human version of the conditioned reflex (Figure 4.2) .

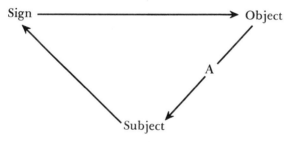

FIGURE 4.2 Signification

Here we deal with simple correlation; one thing heralds another. On the basis of past experience smoke means fire, a smell means rain. In "A" we have signification. All three aspects of meaning—signification, connotation and denotation —may be elicited by any one noise, smell, touch, taste or image. It is the process or response that is critical, not the objective nature of the stimulus.

In social discourse (and usually in thought) symbols are linked in complex fashion, greatly increasing their value as nets to catch the meaning of things. They are related in propositions, which are in Langer's terms, "pictures of structures or states of events." In verbal discourse words stand for concepts standing for experiences of objects and the relations among them. While the "atomic" symbol is a vehicle for meaning, the presentation of symbols in a given order adds to, delimits, and extends that meaning. Thus the symbol "Adam," a proper noun, may refer to almost anything—animal, space project, human. But when we say "Adam is a man," we have greatly increased our information, at the cost of delimiting the meaning of the first symbol. We could go on and add "Adam is a living man," with equally dramatic effects. Thus the units in which we line symbols, and the order of presentation, add meaning. That order is the purview of grammar, out of which logic and semantics have developed.

One may think of a sentence as single but more complex symbol, resting upon many connotations and denotations. As a complex symbol it is analyzable into its constituent parts; these can be studied for implications (and errors) with respect to connotation and denotation of single words, complexes of words, and their order of presentation. Considered as complex single symbols, propositions then evoke general knowledge and past experience in the individual, while sometimes extending that experience through relating the hitherto unknown to the known.

Symbols are, then, Janus-faced in their nature. They have an internal relevance to the individual, based upon their relationship to his past; they have a putative relevance to others. If they are members of a symbol system, a language, shared by a language group, then they have certain delimited social meanings, or probabilities of communication. The more formalized that language, the clearer the symbolic import for others.

But much of our individual experience is symbolized in vague and unstandardized ways. There is, as we say, no word for it. One of the great contributions of creative scientists and artists is to make communicable what was previously moot, to sense those new meanings possible in the emerging nature of human experience, giving them a form which makes communication possible. The phrase-maker is not to be despised; he may be creating the grounds for new social reality. (On the other hand, he may merely be repackaging an old product.)

We *can* communicate by simply pointing to segments of common reality. Primitive communication is possible where the thing itself is meant. Thus in "silent trading" between alien and hostile peoples, one group leaves its goods at night; the other places beside them what it considers equivalent. The first group then accepts the bid or changes its own offering. Such barter occurs without a common language other than the language of objects. But note how clumsy and limited such communication is.

The great power of symbolic communication lies in flexibility and ease of access to past experience with which to confront the new. Symbolized meanings are easier to apprehend and to manipulate than objects; they are easier to combine in larger networks of meaning. They emphasize only the selected aspects of the shared world that matter in the given situation and thus minimize distraction. In this sense, as Langer points out, the most neutral symbolic medium is best; symbols should be things that cannot possibly be confused with the meaning symbolized. The "mouthy little sounds" we call words are ideal: seldom imitative of reality, they are superb evocators of experience.

As a consequence of symbolic discourse man has the freedom to elaborate a constantly expanding network of meaning. He is free to play with meaning, to elaborate and manipulate, to use random search and trial and error in accounting for his individual and collective experience. To be sure, such possibilities of play mean that we easily create "philosophies which Heaven and Earth have never dreamed of." We create the faith in demons, master races, the inevitable triumph of the proletariat, the birth and power of a thousand bloodthirsty gods—or the doctrine that men have fewer ribs than women because of Adam's operation. In short, the possibilities of error are enormously expanded through our symbolific behavior. But the possibility of error is the necessary condition for truth; the range of truth which we may create is expanded proportionately, *pari passu*.

[5]

THE SYMBOLIC ENVIRONMENT
AND PHENOMENOLOGY

Most people do not often consider the aspects of human life we have been discussing. Indeed, many are probably quite unaware of the complex processes that produce the distinctively human vision (some even mistake cats and dogs for people). To them the process of symbolization is as natural as breathing. Symbols are used without understanding their origin or nature and are often confused with the event itself.

Instead of a radical critique of thought, most men live through the practical vision they have inherited from their language group. This is a nondiscursive abstraction of experience, a use of given signs and symbols to move through our maze toward our goals. The given datum is taken as sign plus symbol, and turned into one of the "plain facts" of our life.

Thus a sound is taken as the ringing of a bell, a cue that classes will begin and doors will close. It symbolizes periodicity in our routine, a gathering of persons in a room. The connotations are not necessarily evoked, however; they are there if wanted but, in the given situation, that sensation in the ears is adequate for the act of entering the classroom. Nor are the denotations important; we may casually note the real bell on the wall, but it may be hidden and we may never see it, though it helps us order our behavior a thousand times.

This is the closest we come to animal behavior in our significant actions; it is still very distant from Pavlov's dogs. For we can analyze the structure that leads from the sound

48

to the postulated bell and its connotation. Thus we hear many bells we disregard, and should a trickster ring the right bell at the wrong time, we would know and disregard it. We react *habitually* because we do not need to keep in mind the symbolic structure on which the bell's meaning depends, whereas to react in Pavlovian fashion, a student would have to run to the classroom, something which only the very pathological student is apt to do. The bell is a sign of a fact which is a symbol—standing for a very complex situation that includes such things as the need to attend classes to improve grades and even in some instances the desirability of hearing a professor's lecture.

Nor do we often analyze the structure of meaning that allows our everyday discourse. Our interpretations of the world are judged not by formal logic or rigorous and skeptical inquiry, but by their congruence with the common vocabulary of our culture and specifically our important listeners. "Explanation" is what will be acceptable within the belief system of our important reference groups, "justification" what is acceptable to their moral order. The dialectic of everyday life tends to perpetuate the existing common culture while tinkering with its details.

Paul Radin tells of a Winnebago hunter who, before taking the field, first shot an arrow down an empty path. He explained that this arrow had first to go ahead, find the deer, and kill its spirit; after that had occurred the hunter could then kill the animal's body with another arrow. Nevertheless, in his selection of site and conditions suitable for the physical kill, the hunter drew upon a wealth of practical experience. When Radin asked the Indian whether the preliminary measure would be successful if the arrow were shot down an unfamiliar trail, he received "a prompt and amused denial."

The criterion for validity of the magical act was the belief system and moral order of the group; the criterion for the practical act was the likelihood, on empirical grounds, of felling a deer. Lest this seem too exotic to be relevant, let us remember that Christian congregations both pray to their omnipotent God for the conversion of the heathen and also solicit funds for the purpose of sending missionaries, rice, and bibles to help out. We have a formula to cover such cases: "God helps those who help themselves." In short, some attention must be paid to practicality, even though we are under no compulsion to make it square logically with our other behavior.

The criterion of practical vision in everyday *discourse* is acceptance or rejection by our own kind. Thus the existence of witchcraft was sustained for thousands of years by the practical consensus of people with opinions (so much so that many of the 200,000 witches burned in the sixteenth and seventeenth centuries seem to have shared that belief; there is a sense of importance connected with any role to which power is ascribed). But the criterion of practical vision in *action* is the pragmatic result.

"It works for my purpose" is the empirical validation of practical vision. But what works for one's purpose need not be explicitly conceptualized at any high level of generality. Only that is ordinarily made conscious which is necessary for action. The concepts of practical vision may be compared to recipes, formulae for producing cakes or cannon, while the concepts of science result in chemistry. And indeed, before Mendeleev the practice of chemistry was little more than a vast collection of recipes; in the periodic table he was able to provide a calculus that related them to each other in terms of a more general order (one which explained why recipes worked). But the ordinary housewife obviously has little need for chemistry. If she did we would all have died of starvation or indigestion long ago.

To be sure there are times when the practical actor does worry about contingent laws and the larger framework. This is when he must ask "under what conditions does this work"— generally when the recipe has failed or he faces a new kind of situation. When recipes fail, when the milk in the dairy sours, some explanation is necessary. If it happens only occasionally, explanation is easy in terms of the folk culture— thunder overhead, the leprechauns at night who were not fed, immorality in the household—there are many formulae for dismissing the failure. But if the recipes fail often and the milk is important, it is possible that experiments will occur, although they may be experiments in leprechaun control.

Practical vision, in discourse and in action, is a universal and conservative mode of behavior. It is the routine, the habitual mode of life for most people most of the time. In looking at primitive cultures or the peasant societies of our past, we term it "folk culture." In our own complex and civilized world we call it "common sense." The difference is negligible; common sense is the folk thought of a society viewed by a participant in the society. It is what everyone knows and nobody bothers to question since it works.

Much is made nowadays of the "disenchantment of the world" through the development of science. We see the churches abandoning sharp distinctions of dogma and practices in the light of research—the Bible itself criticized and retranslated, the semitribal allegiance to one truth and one only suffering attrition as ecumenicalism grows, the autonomy and legitimacy of congregations denied, and even the "death of God" discussed by ministers (some eight decades after Nietzsche scandalized Christiandom by remarking it). And in truth, realism or "realityism" does appear to be an important part of the cultural style emerging in the most wealthy and technologically advanced societies.

This realityism is most often explained by the growth of the sciences. For the goal of science as an ideology is the construction of a theory that will imply all the facts of human experience. Objective fact is then the ultimate criterion; all crucial propositions are designed for the ordeal of factual test. Then, from these considerations, it follows that all that cannot be tested is irrelevant to the truth.

But Langer notes that science has probably been less important than history in the disenchantment of the world. It was historians and those hybrids, geologists, with their careful gathering of deposits from the past, who first disproved the sacred myths of the tribe. Their cutting edge was the discovery of causal linkages, linkages of "historical fact" that made fairy tales of what had been taken as literal truth. For historians reinterpret the past in the terms of the present. The geologist determines from the layered earth its age and the age of life, quite unimaginable; the textual analyst discovers that biblical accounts are polyglot in origins, the "book" of some sacred individual a pastiche by many hands over many years. Thus history as the truest account of the past, that which jibes with the evidence in the light of present-day criteria, is a destroyer of myth. It is a creator of comparative cases for social science; the patriarchal family of the ancient Hebrews is compared to surviving forms among the nomads of the Middle East or to the Israeli *kibbutz*.

In the realistic world view, causality itself is the final cause. Both the "natural laws" of science and the "facts of History" are finally creations based upon the assumption of causality, of that which, pushing from behind, produces a given present. But causality is a giant assumption and, as we have already noted, scientifically determined causality an even greater one. Evans-Pritchard tells of a Nuer whose son drowned when his canoe was charged by an angry rhinoceros. The man immediately began to speculate as to which person had used the poison that caused his son's death. When questioned about "poison," in the light of the simple sequence of events (the boy crossed the river, a rhinoceros was especially touchy, their paths met, and the rhino behaved predictably) he simply asked: "Why should that rhino appear at that time and place? It was poison." Thus causality is a way of reducing the uncertainties of life to manageable proportions: our own explanation, random variation and natural law, is hardly more attractive than the Nuer assumption of magic. Both are ways of imputing human meaning, order and purpose, to an inhuman world. They are probably projections onto outer reality of our own sense of purpose.

The doctrine of realism has, however, saturated the high culture of our society. Supernaturalism has declined in all our institutions, including the churches: the antimythic solvent has forced a definition of man as a species, like others, on a small planet in a corner of a minor galaxy. But it has not thereby made men into scientists. Indeed, even the educated person is usually vague about the working process that leads to the findings of the physical and social scientists; he accepts them because of their esthetic beauty or their apparent ineluctability. But he accepts them mostly on faith.

The less educated accept science because of its technological successes, from medical practices to the exploration of outer space. But the intellectual structure of what is accepted is vague or unknown: in a sense, science is another myth for such a person. Causality, taken on faith, is substituted for magic and the supernatural as basic explanation. He knows as little of science as the thirteenth-century peasant knew of formal theology; it is simply a stopping point for what could be an infinite regression.

Indeed, most of us understand most sciences about as well as we understand the processes that allow our automobiles to move at our will. We drive our automobile, as we marry our wife who bakes our cake, by recipes we have learned in the tribe. Practical vision gets us through our lives, and we explain (where we feel it necessary) through realism—the assumption of scientific law, the assumption of historical fact.

Thus our "scientific civilization" does not produce a scientific philosophy. Men are capable of learning, using and creating science during their working day, and worshipping Jehovah on Sunday: physicians may very well be Seventh Day Adventists. For there is no inherent need for close logical fit in our personal philosophy, perhaps a "strain toward consistency" at best. One of the most penetrating themes of Santayana was this capability of humanity both to believe and not believe, depending upon the situation. Or, in the line he made famous, one can believe that "there is no God, and Mary is His mother."

Psychological order in the individual does not conform to the rules of logical order in discourse, as rationality in a social organization does not necessarily produce logical reasoning in the members of that organization. One of the great contributions of the sociology of work has been the discovery, in case after case, of the nonrational behavior of workers and management alike in large-scale highly bureaucratized cor-

porations. There are the familiar stories of the executives
undone because they were assigned an office without a wall-
to-wall carpet. More to the point are the studies of resistance
to technological change by top-level management, even
though it is to the rational good of the enterprise. But what
benefits General Motors may not seem good for the individual employee. Then too, we all show different faces in our
different roles, for no single role includes all of our being; the
research physicist who is on occasion a Sunday School teacher
may or may not feel it necessary to relate these two aspects of
his life in a logical fashion.

SOME METHODOLOGICAL
IMPLICATIONS

In this view, human behavior is forever and inextricably symbolic in its guiding principles. That symbolism may reflect
the use and wont of the culture, its conventional wisdom; it
may reflect recipes based upon highly sophisticated science
without understanding that science; it may reflect the pro-
foundly esthetic in vision, combination and interpretation.
The "rational man," like "political man" and "economic
man," is a highly selective abstraction from the multiverse of
individual systems which interact, cooperate, and contend in
social groups. What is implied for the social scientist?

   The first and most obvious implication is a constraint in
the way he can view his subject matter, social life. If the
meaning of events varies with the individual frame of reference, then the scientist cannot assume that it is consistent for
all participants. The "definition of the situation" becomes a
crucial concern, and W. I. Thomas' observation, that "if
men define a situation as real then it is real in its consequences," is axiomatic. Thus subjective reality, the psychological fields of the social actors, must be assumed to vary. If,
therefore, one thinks this subjective reality is critical to understanding human life, then he must become adept at imag-

inative projection, at taking the standpoint of "the other" and inferring meaning through borrowed frames of reference.

Further, it is clear that the frame of reference varies enormously among societies. Thus one must be extremely cautious in translating the meaning of an act from one society to another. Who loves his aged infirm mother most—the Eskimo who cuts her throat or the American who asks her to live with him? Before we answer we must remember that when an old Eskimo woman's teeth are gone she is useless and will starve to death; knowing this, she prefers the brief pain of violent death to suicide through freezing in a blizzard; a good son will act accordingly. To reverse the emphasis, American officials have had a very difficult time transplanting our "public administration" craft to non-Western countries. Where kinship is king, the rules of bureaucratic order that make our large-scale organizations work predictably turn into a blind for nepotism and "corruption."

Even within societies there are enormous differences in frames of reference. There is, for example, the muted quarrel among social scientists over the true nature of class differences in significant meaning. Schatzman and Strauss, studying reactions to a disaster, note the unorganized and even incoherent reports of poor and uneducated victims, compared to the semantic order and specificity of the middle class. Others argue, however, that the lower class respondents in our society are simply not interested in the same "facts" as the middle class social scientist: they have a rational order and a vocabulary, but they are not available to the middle class frame of reference. Herbert Gans has recently documented life in a working class neighborhood of Boston—a present-centered, social-oriented way of life, quite far from the future-centered, achievement-oriented way common to social scientists. It is clear that whatever the differences in degree of order, there are major differences in the *shape* of order by social class and ethnic background.

Finally, it must be remembered that there can be enormous differences between individual frames of reference in many matters. They can vary by the great social dividers, age and sex. Anthropologists note that even in the simplest societies, nobody knows *all* the cultural tradition: women may be prohibited from knowledge that is a male perquisite, males may simply be unable to take the perspective of the female. The child's point of view is always different, from ignorance if from nothing else. Then, more important, as a society grows complex and differentiated we have variations in perspective growing out of "cultural mutation," different mixes of experience, intellectual and otherwise. With relaxed group controls, all sorts of individual experimenting and innovation are possible; the richness of the cultural materials allows for fantastic combinations and permutations. The sociologist's son becomes an orthodox Jew; the businessman's daughter becomes a devotee of yoga and hashish.

Even those social scientists who are uninterested in "meaning" must take note. Though they are "black box" theorists, who put individual significance as an "X" between stimulus and response, input and output, and solve for X in the simplest fashion, their task will be simplified if they remember that X is a transformer, with powerful patterns of its own, and these vary from X to X in determinable ways.

How, then, we must ask, is any description of an overall social reality possible? If each individual suffers a bias, and a different bias, from his perspective, how can we picture the structure within which they exist? And this new word, "structure," is exactly the point: we must construct a hypothetical set of relationships that *explain* the variation in perspective—in order to understand what the individual is telling us.

It is somewhat like the process of locating a forest fire from a distant smoke. If we have a map locating three fire-watchers relative to each other and the terrain, and if we ask each to locate the smoke from his point of view, we can draw three lines which will intersect and locate the fire on the map in one spot, and one only.

But obviously we need a social map. And equally obviously, we need to know the position of each observer in the structure that map implies. Finally, we need our criterion event, our forest fire (in social research, our race riot, depression, or political assassination). Bias is ubiquitous and unavoidable, for perspectives must differ; the social scientist must, then, *use* that bias in his pursuit of the structure which produces it.

There are also important implications for the relationship between the investigator and his subject matter in the view of man as symbolizer. For one, it is clear that we have several levels of conception to deal with, and they must be clearly defined and separated in our thought. Looking at the simplest social unit, the interaction between two people, there are at least three sharply different levels of discourse.

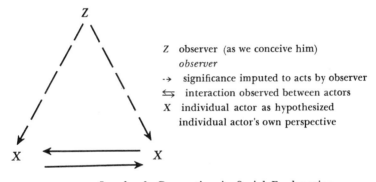

Z   observer (as we conceive him)
     observer
-→   significance imputed to acts by observer
⇆   interaction observed between actors
X   individual actor as hypothesized
     individual actor's own perspective

FIGURE 5.1. Levels of Conception in Social Explanation

In Figure 5.1 X represents the abstractive vision of each actor in the two-person view. As we have seen, this can vary greatly. (One can see a moving fan blade, another a fan at rest.) Then we have the outside observer's inference as to what the situation means to each actor—what he thinks they think. There are many opportunities for error here. Finally, the social scientist assigns the total event significance in his own framework of interpretation, his own social theory. What he can observe and test objectively may be a small part of this.

The scientist's frame of reference is not likely to be the same as that of the actors, but he must translate the meaning he imputes to them into the terms of his own theory. Thus, in the functional explanation of quarrels in marriage, one is concerned not with the object of dispute *per se* but with the way "revealed differences," possible only in anger and the release of an open quarrel, may result in communication useful to the ongoing marital relationship. As to exactly how each participant thought and felt his anger, frustration, hurt—that is forever unknowable, ineffable. But one's theory does not require that he observe that.

There are some important corollaries of these propositions. First, it is clear that you cannot blindly impute to others your own frame of reference without testing for comparability and controlling for differences—not if you value accuracy. One does not ask a semiliterate small businessman running a "Momma and Poppa" corner grocery store to discuss the marginal utility of some inventory. Political scientists cannot assume that the average citizen has their kind of intense interest in the issues of government: the opposite assumption is probably more accurate. Too often we analyze survey results which are produced not by the clear-cut knowledge and preference of the citizen but by his indifference or willingness to oblige.

As a further corollary, one cannot confuse the subject's definition of the situation with that of the social scientist. From the latter point of view the subject probably has absolutely no idea of why he behaved as he did; he is not in the social science business but, usually, merely trying his best to get on. Naïveté here can result in documenting not the nature of leadership in a town (or "Community Power Structure"), but merely folk thought on the subject. To be sure, one may find *clues* to the larger significance of action in the interpretation of self-conscious and reflective subjects, but this is part of the hypothesis-forming process, not the testing process.

PHENOMENOLOGY

One outcome of these considerations has been a school of thought known as "phenomenology." Rather vaguely defined and heterogeneous in practice, those who claim the title have tended to insist that the truth about human behavior can be known only when it includes the conceptions of the actors. Thus the focus is upon individual experience and the coercive- ness of the definition of the situation, with language as the key element tying the individual to the group processes. It is a point of view that insists we keep in mind every element in Figure 3, that we do not substitute numbered assumptions for empirical investigations of human reactions and acts.

Such a position leads, in practice, to an extremely awk- ward framework for inquiry. While it warns us of the danger of omission, it courts the opposite danger of overinclusiveness. For there is a high degree of uniformity in any society's life, produced by outside constraints without much attention to in- dividual variation. One may note the regularity with which most automobile drivers stay on the designated side of the street. Regardless of what this means to them (fear of dan- gerous accidents, of police, of penalties, habit, a "compulsive personality," public spirit) their behavior *en masse* is highly predictable. In the same way, there is enormous uniformity in the use of language, as well as clearly patterned variations.

Thus subjective states of mind may be irrelevant to one's interest in a social situation. Although some argue that one must understand the microscopic before the larger structure is clear, that personality precedes social structure, we must re- member that physics began with the study of planets, balls rolling down inclined planes, the lever—not with subatomic structures. The study of population balance and disbalance may or may not require knowledge of the psychology of sex: the study of a formal organization in action may require that we know only one thing about the individual *qua* individual —the probability that he will conform to the normative structure of the group.

But the "phenomenological" approach has had value for the social sciences. It recalls, for one thing, the complex struc- ture of inference underlying our "social facts," and it is a continual critique and caution against the unwarranted as- sumptions of uniformity that really demand empirical test. For another, in emphasizing the need to tie our general theory down to what is implied in observable behavior of people, including their linguistic descriptions and justification of that behavior, it stimulates return to the empirical occasion, the concrete fact from which our speculations may re-emerge braced with awareness of the complexity and "thereness" of the social world.

[II]

ABSTRACTION AND INNOVATION

[6]

ORIGINS OF SCIENCE

The creation of physical science is perhaps the most spectacular achievement of the human race. Whether we think of it in Robinson Jeffers' terms as "mind like a many-bladed machine devouring the universe," or we see it as lending man a quasi god-like status, the sheer intellectual creation is overwhelming. In its most complete flowering, physics, it is a beautiful and powerful structure. Yet much of that structure was created early in the history of mankind's interest, and with breathtaking speed. Whitehead says:

The whole development of thought occupied exactly two generations. It commenced with Galileo and ended with Newton's *Principia*; and Newton was born in the year that Galileo died. Also the lives of Descartes and Huyghens fall within the period occupied by these great terminal figures. The issue of the combined labours of these four men has some right to be considered as the greatest single intellectual success which mankind has achieved. In estimating its size, we must consider the completeness of its range. It constructs for us a vision of the material universe, and it enables us to calculate the minutest detail of a particular occurrence.

To be sure, men had speculated about such matters as stars, planes, the attraction of the earth, projectiles, for thousands of years. But never before had they developed such powerful understanding.

This achievement, like practical vision, did not require intensive analysis of epistemology. (As Norman Campbell points out: "the great philosophers of science, such as Bacon or Mill, have never been able to apply their rules to the discovery of any law of the slightest value. Laws have been discovered for the most part by people naïvely innocent of all philosophical subtleties.") The world of objects was taken as given and the structure of relationships underlying it built upward. But unlike the common sense of everyday life, that structure was pursued toward closure, a pursuit not oriented to practical goals. The objects were seen in a vast context. In Langer's terms, "practical vision" was put in double harness with the concept-forming and transforming mind: the resulting problems and solutions-become-problems were exposed to the organized energies of an intellectual community. The criteria of achievement were simple but awesome in their implications: Law must lead to facts in stubborn interrelations and facts must be exemplification of precisely formulated law.

It required a massive faith in the order of the universe. And as we have noted, that faith is larger than and prior to science, an assumption leading to science as one conclusion. We find such order, and faith in order, in the tragedies of the Greeks, for in tragedy each act exemplifies law and law is grounded in event. Tragedy is based on the inexorable. But the scientific vision knows the inexorable all around us and spells it out in the interrelations of Blake's "minute particulars" of experience.

Whitehead sees this faith developing out of vast cultural trends in the history of Western man. In the thought of the fifth-century Greeks we find the first development of a strictly secular cosmology, free of both arbitrary mystery and the whims of supernatural beings. Perhaps the Greek *polis,* with its insistence on a humanly understandable process of government and an accountable rule, lay at its basis. In such a scheme authority was finally the result of a dialectic among a community, logic the tool for finding the truth. Certainly the Greeks were concerned to bring the exigencies of the world into a meaningful order, as in the play where Aeschylus brings the wild daemonic protectors of the blood lineage, the furies, into the Athenian *polis* where they become citizens— "the Kindly Ones."

But the Greek stance was basically dramatistic. They were

interested in final causes, in what things were for, in purpose. To them it was clear that fish had fins in order to swim, for the cause of anything was given in its effects. Rather than seeing the world as being urged on from behind to the given event, they saw the event itself as an explanation for the process which gave it birth. Their supremely social orientation led them to project the human community and its purposes upon the world at large. Because they were interested in the ends of action and tended to accept the means as given they were weak in patient observation, muddled suspense, inductive reasoning. Empirically, they held to the practical vision; in speculation they roamed a symbolized cosmology. The two were not necessarily considered together and usually logic, not controlled experiment, was the discipline for resolving theoretical disputes.

Yet the achievement of a few hundred men was dazzling. The formalization of logic was a triumph. The development of geometry, an enterprise combining logical rigor, mathematical precision, and empirical predictability, created a basic paradigm for science. Taken together with the pioneering efforts of Aristotle in the biological and social sciences, they constitute the historical origins of a great many contemporary fields of inquiry.

Underlying the achievement was a tough-minded external view of the world. Even after the decline of Greece into a minor Roman province that view persisted in the philosophy of stoicism, a secular religion of the elite. It became objectively embodied in the order and structural integrity of Roman law, which continued to light the intellectual horizons as an afterglow long past the demise of the Roman state. Indeed, the example of that law was important in the growing development of scholastic philosophy, an enterprise which aimed at nothing less than spelling out all law for all humanity.

The primitive tribal God of the Hebrews, the anthropomorphic Father of the primitive Christians, was greatly transformed by the learned philosophers of the Church. As He became Romanized, His will was seen as the source of an authority that was lawful, itself law-enforcing, and objectively rational in its details, a system of organization. If He sees the sparrow fall and the details of the conscience, then His order pervades the universe: it is in no sense anarchic, disorderly, whimsical.

The world view of the scholastics was, like that of the Greeks, intensely dramatistic. But now the drama was different: the major theme was not success at the pursuits of men or the winning of civic glory, but salvation of the immortal soul in the conflict between good and evil. As Randall put it:

> The world was a great allegory, whose essential secret was its meaning, not its operation or its causes; it was a hierarchical order, extending from lowest to highest, from stones and trees through man to the choirs upon choirs of angels. . . . From the highest heaven to the lowest clod, aspiration to fulfill the will of God, to blend with the divine purpose, was the cosmic force that made the world go round.

Such a cosmology is closer to that of classical China than to our present views. Indeed, with its explanation of significance and its disregard for concrete physical detail, it could have lasted indefinitely. It is a variation on the great myths of origin and destination which everywhere preceded the scientific awakening.

Why then did it die? At the beginning of the sixteenth century the wars of religion were the dominant concerns. The successful crusade of His Most Catholic Majesty, the King of Spain, had just vanquished Moors and Jews alike. By the end of the seventeenth century the medieval world view was in collapse and classical physics had been created. But physics did not topple the medieval synthesis; one might better say that the exhaustion of that world view allowed for the rise of the scientific sensibility. The title of Huizinga's study, "The Waning of the Middle Ages," is a dramatic statement; a great civilization was dying. Christendom was going under and in the reviving cities men were inspecting the concrete details of their life in a new frame of reference.

From the Christian world view there remained a great legacy, however: faith in order. There was the belief that, in Whitehead's words, "Every detailed occurrence can be correlated with its antecedents in a perfectly definite manner exemplifying general principles." But the nature of the general principles had changed from the will of God to the relationships and structures of the physical universe.

The dramatistic stance was abandoned, once and for all. One did not look for final causes but for efficient ones—those that allowed prediction in terms of contingency, temporal or spatial. The question "Why?" changed to the question "How?" And with the increasing success of mathematical statements of relationship, the question became "How much?" The "Newtonian World-Machine," as Randall called it, answered a great many questions of this kind. Our experiences are produced by our contact with a vast encompassing order which behaves with machinelike precision and is predictable and explicable through a knowledge of its laws.

Notably, the laws were conceived as *of this outer order,* though "discovered" by the scientists. Thus the medieval synthesis, which rested upon allegory (and encouraged an orgy of symbolization), was turned inside out. Order moved from inside the soul to "out there." To be sure, there were certain intellectual puzzles implied: if the cause is not given in its effect but simply precedes it predictably, one cannot really prove causation. As a corollary, logical proof is quite independent of empirical test and cannot be accepted as adequate for matters of fact—a further weakening of the scholastic methods.

Such problems did not really worry the men who were creating the physical sciences. They combined a strong suspicion of the inner order (stated for them by Bacon) with a great faith in the outer order, the world of stubborn fact. Thus we can say that science was, in its inception, basically antirational; it proceeded from success to success although unable to explain philosophically why this was possible. But success in these pragmatic terms is evidence of validity for just as long as it continues, and within the limits where it works; beyond these limits it is irrelevant. A great physicist on the nature of God is as irrelevant as a great divine on the nature of physics. (One might mention what has been termed the "Rickover phenomenon"—the mistaking of children in school for submarines.) In a few words, the antirationalism of empirical physical science is a bias, one that continues and so represents a limitation.

The world view that emerged was that of scientific materialism. It was a conception of the world as matter pushed around by laws. Whitehead puts it concisely:

There persists . . . the fixed scientific cosmology which presupposes the ultimate fact of an irreducible brute matter, or material, spread throughout space in a flux of configurations. In itself such a material is senseless, valueless, purposeless. It just does what it does do, following a fixed routine imposed by external relations which do not spring from the nature of its being.

Such a frame of reference directed attention to things useful for solving the problems of interest to the physical scientist— the abstractions were adequate for his concerns. The result was methodological success in dealing with what was abstracted from the flow of human experience. A great order was revealed in certain aspects of the physical world.

"THE FALLACY OF MISPLACED CONCRETENESS"

For two-and-a-half centuries science lived on the "accumulated capital of ideas provided . . . by the genius of the seventeenth century." It was a genius oriented toward physics, a science dominated by the accomplishments of physicists. It was not particularly suitable for the biological and social sciences, and the latter in particular got off to a series of false starts through analogizing from physics. Hobbes attempted to analyze the political structure of the state by physical metaphor and ended up with a predictable emphasis upon force. (It was after all a concept common to both politics and physics.) Quetelet attempted to create a "social physics" of population. To be sure, such efforts were not totally wasted; the insights of Hobbes and the development of social statistics by Quetelet were not mean achievements. But when we compare such results to those of Galileo and Newton they are disappointing.

The difficulty seemed to lie in the antirationalism of science. For the use of practical vision, the acceptance of objects at their common-sense significance in order to demonstrate lawful relations among them did not work in social science. Configurations of population did not lawfully and precisely produce new configurations; even in breeding and dying human beings were not mere bodies pushed around by simple laws. Certainly the common-sense definitions of force in politics were inadequate as explanations of the birth, growth, change and death of states.

The abstractions that worked in physical science were inadequate to the social scientists. But this was *the* scientific frame of reference they knew. And a frame of reference can be a rigid constraint, a blinder producing "tunnel vision." How then does one escape it? Whitehead has two suggestions. First, we can improve our sense data and use it to criticize the frame; second, we can make greater theoretical demands upon the frame, comparing it to other schemes of abstraction based upon valid experience—demanding, thereby, a larger order. Neither is easy.

But the appeal to concrete experience is the more popular solution. Since Bacon's revolt against deduction, it has been generally believed that with "sufficient care in the collection of instances the general law would stand out." But induction does not, as we have seen, begin without preconceived notions; indeed, they will determine what instances you collect—so that the nature of concrete instances is actually deduced from some prior theoretical frame of reference (probably of a folk, or common sense, variety). True induction must be through experiences which jolt the conceptual framework; Whitehead notes that "the key to the process of induction . . . is to be found in the right understanding of the immediate occasion in its *full concreteness*." This concreteness can only mean in aspects not given by the framework which led you to select it.

Unimaginative empiricism, in which one simply collects cases in terms of a sterile framework, is not only unprofitable; it may be a barrier to discovery. Thus the pre-Galilean physicist assumed that bodies are naturally at rest until acted upon by a force, a view that accords well with common sense. Galileo's great achievement was made possible by changing that assumption to this: bodies at rest remain at rest and bodies in motion continue in motion in a straight line unless acted upon by outside forces. Such a little shift in assumptions held enormous implications.

In the social sciences the analogous shift was from the belief that societies are naturally stable (at rest) until acted upon by "outside forces." Today we assume that all societies change but that the *rate of change* varies with internal and external conditions: Marx helped us to see the apparently stable present as a precarious balance of forces at many levels. Thus the typical view that social disorganization is an anomaly which must be accounted for is reversed in contemporary sociology. The interesting question is: What are the conditions for *organization*. Societies may be "naturally" organized or disorganized, as men may be "naturally" sane or mad. Such considerations represent major shifts in assumptions, away from folk thought or common sense.

Classical physics assumes that simple location, the existence of a body of some mass in a given place, is the primary aspect of reality. Such "qualities" as color and smell are peculiar to people and are not there in nature; therefore they are not real. Simple location is the only reality. But in truth this suppression amounts to a value judgment: the physical abstraction of the world (simple location) is "real" for the physicist because it is efficient for his problems; it works. His abstractions—time, space, mass—result from the suppression of other details in experience; purpose lies behind that suppression.

Both "qualities" and "essentials" are equally abstractions from the concrete instance. In the enormous success of physical science men tended to elevate its notions of the essential to an adequate picture of human reality. Thus the peculiar anguish of the Victorians; what was real was indifferent to any question of morality, and esthetics was a subject dealing with one's own sensorium.

Each molecule blindly runs. The human body is a collection of molecules. Therefore, the human body blindly runs, and therefore there can be no individual responsibility for the actions of the body.

So Whitehead puts the dilemma. It left one without freedom, moral responsibility, or self-respect. Most of what mattered in human life was trivial, reduced to the status of epiphenomena.

Once we have recognized the extremely abstract nature of the physical view of experience, however, the solution to the puzzle is clear.

the whole concept of materialism only applies to very abstract entities, the products of logical discernment. The concrete enduring entities are organisms, so that the plan of the *whole* influences the very character of the various subordinate organisms which enter into it. . . . The electron blindly runs . . . within the body; that is to say, in accordance with the general plan of the body, and this plan includes the mental state.

The eminent Victorians suffered through substituting the abstracted aspects of interest to the scientist for the concrete instances, the events of their experiences. This is what Whitehead calls the fallacy of misplaced concreteness. But their despair was itself a factor in the way their molecules ran. As Mencius asks, "Is it any different to kill a man with a stick than with a sword? And is it any different to kill him with a false philosophy than with a stick?"

The view of man as social actor and as social scientist that I am stating here is pluralistic. There are many levels of order discernible in our behavior, from the rigid constraints of the body (legs usually bend backward at the knee) to the rigid constraints of custom and law. Within these constraints, however, there remains a great and generally increasing room for variation in thought and action. The results of this variation feed back upon the person and determine the next state of being, the next event. We can call this a degree of freedom or, acting upon faith, believe it is inexorably determined (though by events which we do not, personally, understand) .

Blake's response to the intellectual imperialism of physics was written long before Whitehead, yet the positions are similar:

> The Atoms of Democritus
> And Newton's Particles of Light
> Are sands upon the Red Sea shore,
> Where Israel's tents do shine so bright.

Of course there is order in the world, but we do not extend our understanding of it by taking one abstrative scheme as definitive for all aspects of events. The Fallacy of Misplaced Concreteness is exactly that sort of error.

[7]

ABSTRACTION, ANALYSIS,
AND SYNTHESIS

The process of abstraction is, then, double-edged. It is extremely useful if it is well founded, if it corresponds with those aspects of the world in which we are interested. It allows us to avoid distraction by means of what is called "partial analysis," and if what we are interested in is itself relatively free from distraction, we are in a good position to understand it. But there is a price; you have excluded parts of a whole, and if those parts excluded are important in your concerns then you have built in a major error.

Although there is in human experience a continuous and organic interplay between conception and response to the world, it is useful to distinguish them. Let us call the former "the conceptual realm," the latter "the spatio-temporal continuum." The first is the set of ideas described in various philosophies as "the realm of possibility," "universals," or "eternal objects." In the metaphysical framework they refer to all that we could imagine, as contrasted with the limited and arbitrary nature of what indeed is. Here we will simply consider the conceptual realm as the concepts available for possible application to events in the ongoing spatio-temporal continuum.

The conceptual realm is concretized in language, but only partly so. Concepts, after all, precede words, and individual conceptions precede concepts. There are those individuals who conceptualize not in verbal but in spatial terms, finding speech difficult, writing a very clumsy method of formulation and communication. There are also the concepts of the artists, which usually precede any verbal interpretation and are often quite impossible to paraphrase verbally.

The conceptual realm, like individual concepts, has both a psychological and a logical status. The logical status is implicit in the community, the social interchange and storage system that makes the thoughts of others, alive or dead, available to us. The psychological is manifest in the freedom with which anyone can approach the existing systems of thought and reinterpret, explore, infer and in general innovate. This is possible because the individual is a system, having a memory and a symbolizing capacity. (Otherwise innovation could result only from mistakes in the society or from outside forces.) The two kinds of system, the psychological individual and the social logic, forever interact; they produce intellectual history.

But the conceptual realm is not in fact unitary. It is fragmented and variable, by societies and cultures and periods of civilization, by individual variation and invention. Its existence at any given point in time reflects what has been discovered or created and kept as having some possible value for individual or group. But with the increasing interaction of men over the entire globe and with the sifting of concepts and selection of those which, being more generally relevant, are more enduring, it is likely that the conceptual realm is moving toward a true "universality," at least for this species on this small planet. We are acculturating to the human race.

It has been said that concepts are relational in their essence. By this we mean that they relate the given event to other events not present, and relate the responding being to a stimulating environment. They turn a red sphere on a branch into a (hypothesized) apple, from which one can generalize to other aspects of apple—edibility, taste, the botanical niche, and so on.

But another, and equally important, meaning of this "relational essence" is the sense in which all concepts are relatable to each other. They coexist in a formal world, where each has a status *vis à vis* the others, even though it be merely

"no known relationship at present." (The fact of unrelated-
ness may be an important aspect of the given concept.) Thus
to explain a concept we have to go beyond it with still other
concepts—unless we relate directly to the object through
pointing.

At an extreme we have concepts which are defined *only*
by their relations with others. In mathematics such concepts
are the rule. Thus:

$$(A+B)^2 = A^2 + 2AB + B^2$$

Beyond such relations as these, mathematical concepts add
nothing; each term is a function of each other term.

We can imagine a seamless web of conceptual linkages. It
might be described, analogically, in this fashion:

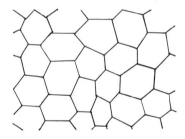

Each concept is defined by the limits placed upon it by others,
each shares all of its walls and has no separate identity. Thus
we might take the apparently simple concept, "social group,"
and attempt to define it accurately. Group implies individual
components, social implies mutual modification in discernible patterns of interaction among individuals over time. Each
term implies opposites, analogies, a complex conceptual system. *Relationships with other concepts are internal to the
very identity of the given concept.*

This raises what is sometimes called "the problem of context." As Whitehead puts it:

The difficulty which arises in respect to internal relations is to
explain how any particular truth is possible. In so far as there are
internal relations, everything must depend upon everything else.

But if this is the case, we cannot know about anything till we equally know everything else. Apparently, therefore, we are under the necessity of saying everything at once. This supposed necessity is palpably untrue. Accordingly, it is incumbent on us to explain how there can be internal relations, seeing that we admit finite truths.

The solution is, simply, partial analysis. We can discuss a particular relation among given concepts without any reference to other relations except the assumption "that they have, each of them, the requisite status to play their respective role in that multiple relationship." In short, we assume they are either internal to this specific proposition, or else irrelevant to it in the immediate analysis. Some of the most important controversy in social science arises at just this point: what is "internal" to a theory, what is irrelevant to it?

In economic analysis does one have to include the psychology of consumer behavior? In organizational research, the personality of the foreman? It depends upon, first, how important such variables are in influencing the system in question, and, second, how fine a description, explanation, and prediction is wanted. The assumption of a perfect vacuum has been useful in physics although it can only be approximated experimentally. In the same fashion, the economist can say that, in large numbers of cases variations in consumer behavior "average out" as powerful factors and can be disregarded. Or they can be summarized and made internal to his theory in the form of "demand lag" or "random fluctuation," those aspects relevant to his problem. But the partial nature of one's analysis is, again, a function of his purpose.

ABSTRACTIVE HIERARCHIES

Conceptualizing is a process of abstracting, and concepts are inherently abstract. Though, as Whitehead says, we present ourselves with "simplified editions of immediate matters of fact . . . they are in truth only to be justified as being elaborate logical constructions of a high degree of abstraction." We have discussed the symbolization process earlier; let us now look at the products, the concepts native to any conceptual realm.

At one extreme we have concepts which are simple; they cannot be broken down into necessary parts. A given color is such a concept. These are the conceptualized elements of the differentiated esthetic continuum. They are known variously as "primitives," "atomic facts," or "simple concepts." Such a concept is just itself; it functions as a pointer and/or as a component in more complicated networks of meaning.

When we start combining simple concepts we can create increasingly complex ones. Thus when we add "A" and "B" in any relationship we have a higher "grade" concept, $R(AB)$, one which has three terms and which, taken as a whole, is a complex statement. So we can combine a color (red) and a shape (round) and move toward a first approximation of what may end as "apple"—a very complex concept. So each complex concept stands at the peak of a pyramid of meaning; in Whitehead's terms, it connotes an "abstractive hierarchy."

Contrariwise one can analyze a complex concept down to its constituent parts through decreasing grades of complexity. The notion of a "social group" leads finally to the sense data taken as standing for (1) individuals (2) behavior (3) modification, qualified by (4) mutuality and (5) endurance (which is really (6) repetition in (7) a context of change, or "reiteration"). It also leads to concepts of relationship, not given by the sense data but applied to it by inference: these are indivisible relational concepts—being–nonbeing, together–apart.

With a consistent and valid abstractive hierarchy we should be able to descend to specific and determinate observations. Things should be, in observation, just *so* if we are correct in our analysis and the concept (say, social group) is applicable to the event. However, when we start with the event the reverse does not hold; there are an infinite number of abstractive hierarchies possible when we begin with the simple concepts. This is because we can change the significance of the simplest data through the frame of reference we bring to play: not only those of the artist, moralist, theologian, philosopher or scientist of various sorts, but also those frameworks which we have forgotten, which we have not yet developed, and which we cannot imagine.

This apparently esoteric aspect of abstraction has a hard-bitten corollary. While a given theory (or abstractive hierarchy) can demand that the events be such and so and is falsified if they are not, a given configuration of events does not demand any particular theory. Thus it is forever possible to disprove our theory but not, finally, possible to prove it. (Quite often two or more theories fit adequately the same events.) This is to repeat, at another level, our earlier point: science is in its essence hypothetical, the best guess for the moment. To make it more would require a survey of all possible abstractive hierarchies, but since these are infinite in number the task would be forever incomplete. The best we can do is keep this particular aspect of interpretation in mind and test alternative abstractions as we discover them. To repeat, no description can exhaust empirical reality; conceptual hierarchies, however complex, are always description couched in a given frame of value.

The difference between the conceptual realm and the spatio-temporal continuum is sometimes termed the "analytic" versus the "synthetic." The analytic, as its name implies, deals with abstract forms and their relations; it is the conceptual realm regarded as pure theory. In it anything at all is possible within a chosen (or involuntary or given) order, though contradiction is not acceptable in most systems. As against the analytic we have the synthesis of conceptual and spatio-temporal in our ongoing career through space-time: this is the synthetic. Here the two realms meet and fuse in the event.

There is in their very nature considerable lack of fit between the conceptual realm and the spatio-temporal. We can conceptualize many things that never were, and the world of ongoing experience includes much of which we stand in ignorance. Hamlet was right, and our reversal of Hamlet equally right; there are more things on earth than in our philosophy, and more things in our philosophy than on earth. But the two realms come together in that synthesis we call experience.

The given event is the harsh editor of our concepts, limiting those which are applicable. Thus the great epics of science, the "crucial experiments," are occasions when the applicability of a concept is decided: the abstractive hierarchy proposes, events dispose.

This continual editing of thought by empirical experience creates the value of our theory. For as Whitehead says: "An event is decisive in proportion to the importance (for it) of its untrue propositions; their relevance to the event cannot be dissociated from what the event is in itself by way of achievement." Thus the difference between truth and error. For without conceptualization there is no truth—merely mistakes in adjusting to the given situation. The limitations on conceptualization, however, imposed by the event also create the value, the unique character of that event. It is a crystallization of all that could be in what, for us, is.

There are two kinds of abstraction, and it is worthwhile to remember the difference. (If ignored it can confuse discourse.) First, there is abstraction from the *event*, the esthetic suppression of detail, conceptual and otherwise. We have discussed this in mysticism, where one empties his mind in contemplation; in abstract painting, where one deliberately seeks a new vision. Something similar happens with the physicist who notes only matter in simple location. This can be called descriptive abstraction.

The second meaning of abstraction is when we limit possible interpretations. It is abstraction from the conceptual realm of possibility, by which we reject alternatives in order to choose. This can be called interpretative abstraction.

Thus the simplest, most primitive descriptive concept tells us the least about any actual event, though it may tell us a great deal about interpretation—as in physics. Contrariwise, the most complex descriptive concept tells us the most, for it limits our possibility of conceptualizing the situation. Ruling out a host of alternative conceptions, the more complex the concept the more it focuses straitly upon a given detailed description. Thus one could observe a certain sequence of events and describe it at the primitive level as colored bodies in motion. Here a great many possibilities are not foreclosed (physical propositions often resemble this form). On the other hand, if one describes this same sequence of events as a professional football game in Dallas, Texas, one has narrowed possibility enormously. Of course, if we go too far with such description we have a very unwieldy structure whose interpretation is difficult to generalize to other events. One of the critical choices in scientific theory construction is that between extensive description, which leaves too much in, and a spare analysis, which may leave too much out.

AN EXERCISE IN ABSTRACTION: ARE GROUPS REAL?

A question frequently raised goes to the very foundations of social science: What is the reality status of social groups? Those who raise the question usually have a basically esthetic and ethical problem in mind. They will report that they do not *feel* groups as objects. Groups are not material entities but simply interactions of individuals. Since this is so, the individual is obviously the real unit and the group a mere aspect of individual behavior. The implications lead then to a purely psychological interpretation of human life.

This view of society is an extension of the physical metaphor, materialism. We must ask what we mean by *real?* To repeat, it is what produces enduring patterns accessible to us but not completely controllable by us. We can speak of the order of atoms in a molecule bound with an electrical impulse, the order of molecules equally bounded, and the material result—a stone or a star. The skeptics of social groups are usually satisfied with the reality of such objects.

The reiterations of patterned behavior among a bounded set of people is exactly the same form of unit. We know that unit, contemplatively, when we observe a game, a party, or a World War. We know it in more immediate experience when we violate the rules of the game, when we are exposed to the punishment of the group. The difficulty seems to be in part the physical separateness of people; I would call attention to the relative distances between particles in nuclear physics as much greater. A further difficulty seems to lie in the periodicity of groups: they are together and then not together. But in truth it is not physical proximity that matters— it is the dependability of behavior ordered in a larger discernible pattern which counts. That order is so objective that it allows us to put men in outer space. In short, groups are as real as the interdependence of their parts. In this respect they are not at all different from stones and stars. They are as real as rock; rocks are as unreal as groups.

Groups are abstractions. They are ways of conceiving the interactions of human bodies over time; most people are so much a part of the group structure of society that they have never really examined it. Only as our social life requires increasingly sophisticated knowledge of group structure do we create and broadcast a common-sense sociology appropriate to an organizational society. That sociology should emphasize the abstract character of groups in order to prevent the error opposite to "individualism"—the reification of the group as the one description of human behavior.

CORRECTLY PLACED CONCRETENESS

I have found it a useful procedure to ask students, at some point in this discussion, to formulate both the "fallacy of misplaced concreteness" and the nature of a "correctly placed concreteness." It is an endeavor with no single true answer; it resembles, to some subjects, that Zen Buddhist discipline wherein the teacher asks an unanswerable question and if he does not like the answer (or gets none) raps his protégé over the head with a pole.

But in truth the answer depends finally upon purpose. For we must ask "correctly placed for what?" I think of three different criteria. First, we can see correctly placed concreteness as that abstraction out of the flux of experience which is most efficient for our purposes in *knowing*. This is the methodological level, and it is important: it is a very narrow relevance, however, if it is all we accept.

Intellectually, correctly placed concreteness is a notion that helps us keep in mind the danger of reification. It leads to a healthy respect for the limits of any analytical scheme and protects us against taking analytical principles as exhaustive of synthesis—as reality. Thus it allows us to use the concept of the social group in explaining and predicting human behavior, while avoiding the fallacy of taking "group life" to describe all human experience. It reminds us that groups are hypothesized, analytical tools used in inference.

And at the broader, humane level, the correct placement of concreteness helps us to keep in mind the abstraction itself. For it is as "real" as anything else and worthy of respect; it can be very creative, very dangerous. At the same time it encourages us to return, continually, to the naïve engagement of our sensibility with the world; to an experience that is concrete because it is not completely captive to the abstractive frame with which we view it. This is particularly important in a scientific–technological civilization, where powerful knowledge is highly specialized knowledge, creating professionals whose frame of reference is far from that of the general.

The situation has its dangers. It produces minds in a groove. Each profession makes progress, but it is progress in its own groove. Now to be mentally in a groove is to live in contemplating a given set of abstractions. The groove prevents straying across country, and the abstraction abstracts from something to which no further attention is paid. But there is no groove of abstractions which is adequate for the comprehension of human life. Thus in the modern world, the celibacy of the medieval learned class has been replaced by a celibacy of the intellect which is divorced from the concrete contemplation of the complete facts.

Of course the facts are never "complete." But correctly placed concreteness is the process of continuously expanding meaning and, therefore, concreteness.

[8]

FORMAL LOGIC

Logic is pre-eminently a way of dealing with language. It allows us to objectify our verbal symbols and thus clarify the meanings of words, propositions, and those interlinked propositions called arguments. Thus it is appropriate to begin by considering the several meanings that the term "logic" itself has accumulated, for they should be kept separate.

Anthropological linguists such as Benjamin Lee Whorf have analyzed the grammar and vocabulary, the language behavior, of societies and abstracted the rules for meaning. These may be termed the "folk logic," the empirically observable rules of meaning for that society. They may or may not be consistent with our norms for analysis, but we look for what works in the discourse of that society—the order of communication, the nature of the "clinching argument" in confrontation.

Closely akin to this meaning is the study of various enterprises within a society. One may describe and analyze the set of presuppositions and methods, the "reasoning" underlying some activity and speak of this as a logic (as, "The Logic of Social Inquiry"). Such an inquiry is simply empirical, and we describe the "logic of the humanities" or at another pole, "the logic of childhood games." We imply an order, a linguistic system, however confused, tacit, or incomplete; it is given unity by the social behavior it patterns and reflects.

The more limited connotation is that of "formal logic." This is the study among a scientific community, logicians, of the rules of discursive reasoning, the results of that study, and their application to given verbal statements. It is empirical in that close attention is paid to the language in use, but it is also normative, with a heavy emphasis upon "right reasoning." (A logician is usually a moralist at heart, with a blood-lust to expose "error" and a love of hard, constraining rules.) It is sometimes said that logic is nothing but the study of language, an offshoot of grammar, but if we remember Langer's discussion of language as symbol, that "nothing but" is not so great a limit.

The creation of a symbolic map corresponding to an area of experience is the aim of an empirical science. Such a map is not to be confused with its subject matter; like a geographical map, it is isomorphic with only selected aspects of that world of experience—it has *analogous form*. Thus, the scientific map helps us see, clearly and precisely, the relations between given points, given kinds of events, while it necessarily loses much detail in the process. Everything cannot be said at once. (Indeed, everything cannot be said.)

The maps that we create have no necessary accuracy because there is no independent faculty in us for judging accuracy apart from empirical test. Yet a logically minded person can analyze an argument and disclose error, even though he knows little or nothing about the subject matter. If you say: "Northern Calabash Indians have two heads: This Indian has one head: Therefore this Indian is a Northern Calabash Indian," you will be caught by such a person. This ability to analyze a conceptual structure and detect error, combined with our lack of ability to judge empirical accuracy from the structure alone, gives a clue to the uses and nature of logic. (There are no such things as Northern Calabash Indians, nor, so far as is known, have they ever existed.)

THE USES OF LOGIC

The function of formal logic is to clarify meaning through the study of the forms in which it is stated. It is an application of the dictum: the disorderly nature of the world does not oblige us to have a disorderly mind. Logic, in its broadest sense, allows us to analyze all the implications of our assumptions. This is the power behind Marx's observation that historical determinism is not a streetcar you take as far as you like and then get off: one does not invent an escape from the inescapable.

It sometimes happens that a rigorous analysis of assumptions makes empirical research redundant. Marx's particular form of historical determinism (or "historicism" as it is sometimes called) postulates a history which, through conflict between opposing forces, will eventually result in the proletarian revolution and the withering away of the State. But it is also assumed that one cannot tell just when these events will occur and thus it is impossible to subject the notion to test: they may be always "in the future." (This is a general characteristic of prophecy, which should usually be read as aspiration and not empirical theory.) In social science such propositions are neither true nor false; they are simply meaningless.

A further use of logic is the articulation of the parts of an argument. The abstractive hierarchies are analyzed and their parts made explicit. The argument, the interconnected set of propositions, can then be critically evaluated and qualified, amended or discarded. Thus the argument that Negroes should not have equal rights because they do not have equal intelligence can be considered (without any empirical data), along these terms: (1) Every citizen with less than median intelligence is unequal and should not have equal rights; (2) Half of the population has less than median intelligence (by definition of median) and should not have equal rights; (3) The remaining half will itself have a "median" intelligence and therefore half of this half will be of unequal intelligence and deserve unequal rights: (4) Toward zero. There is obviously some proposition missing in the argument as generally stated.

The clarification of assumptions and the articulation of arguments are carried out through linguistic analysis. That is, we spell out the rules of language and meaning, rules of identity and transformation. By identity we mean at least

that terms should retain their connotation throughout an
argument; thus if the word "group" means at one time an
arithmetical sum (say, all of the electricians counted in the
census reports) and at another time a social class, with all
its rights and duties, inbreeding and organized interests (say,
the "electrician class"), we shall confuse discourse hopelessly.
Even worse, empirical research will resemble verbal juggling:
the rabbit mysteriously appears and disappears, "groups"
come and go at the will of the scientist.

By transformation we mean that the complex concept can
be expanded into its constituent parts. Contrariwise, it can
be contracted into the single term, the "shorthand" for an
entire hierarchy. Thus we can substitute a more detailed definition for a single term in an argument, frequently with
surprising results. Thus:

"Life results in the survival of the fittest."

Fittest = those who have survived, therefore substitute:

"Life results in the survival of those who have survived."

And contrariwise, sometimes the substitution of a summary
term for what had been a complex statement allows us to
see, among a cluster of complex concepts, relations that would
otherwise have been obscure.

The use of complex concepts as shorthand, standing for
many concepts in a given order, is a most common source of
error. When we say "John loves Mary" we are proposing a
relationship between two entities, continuing over some period
of time; but if we confuse words with things we may very
well ask "What is this thing called love?" And in an example
Santayana used with devastating effect, we may say "Alcohol is
intoxicating," as though the liquid in the bottle sat there
in a state of drunken stupor. In both cases we have substituted
a single term for the abstract hierarchy and then been taken
in by our own substitute, treating the complex concept as
simple. (Of course when alcohol is combined with certain
kinds of organisms in certain ways certain effects are likely.)
There is no harm in such shorthand; our discourse would

be very awkward if we did not use it. The important point is a recognition of its nature and the ability to analyze (in case we are really misusing the term in question) its constituent meanings.

Such analysis leads us to unearth hidden assumptions. A major contribution of social science has been the detailed description of cultural variability, for in that variability lies the cause of hidden assumptions that easily invalidate theories of human behavior. Freud's theories of the Oedipal complex, originating in the family drama and determining the son's ambivalence toward his father, rested upon a host of culturally specific assumptions about authority and affection in the nuclear family. Malinowski, in studying the very different society of the Trobriand Islanders, demonstrated just how much of Freud's theory was a "special" one, applicable only when the biological father had authority in the family—that is, when certain assumptions about the family held. In the process, Freud's theories were greatly extended empirically, became more abstract analytically, and changed dramatically. As long as Freud and his colleagues all studied the same family system in the same culture, they took for granted the authority of the biological father; it is extremely difficult *not* to accept the cultural order surrounding and conditioning you from birth. It is like studying whales from inside the belly of the whale. Malinowski's comparative data dramatized variation; his logical analysis found some missing assumptions. Theory profited.

Logical analysis can also unearth hidden contradictions in our assumptions. The early years of this century saw a vogue for explanation of human behavior in terms of "instincts." Racialism, encouraged by the Darwinian theory of evolution, was the framework for extensive lists of "racial instincts," of which the most important was a postulated "instinct for survival." Wars were explained by an "instinct for dominance." The difficulty with such explanations lay in the fantastic variability of human behavior; the list of instincts began to resemble an infinite list of the acts and reactions of men. Thus the esthetic charm of explaining all behavior by a limited number of "basic instincts" was vitiated by empirical evidence. The solution lay in a re-examination of the meaning of instinct; with instincts defined in Darwinian fashion as inherited and nonmodifiable, it became apparent that almost none of our actions are instinctual. Habits, the results of learning, seem closer to the point while the accurate reference of the word "instincts" is to a habit that lies so deep that we are not consciously aware of having learned it.

While hidden assumptions and contradictions may underlie the basic assumptions or postulates of an argument, they are equally possible in the steps of derivation. A very common error is using the same word with different meanings, thus violating the rule of identity. Equally confusing is the practice of using different words for the same meaning. Logical analysis, ferreting out the identities in discourse, can frequently simplify an argument—sometimes to the point where it disappears in verbal circularity (as with the survival of the survivors) .

To summarize, the function of logic is to analyze the implication of the postulates and to articulate the parts of the argument. This is accomplished through spelling out the rules of language and meaning—rules of identity and transformation, expansion, contraction, and substitution. The purpose is to clarify the meanings of propositions and thus to unearth hidden assumptions, implications, and contradictions in postulates and the steps of derivation.

THE NATURE OF LOGIC

Logic cannot give the initial postulates of a theory. These are concepts created otherwise, intuitively given out of the symbolizing and conceptualizing processes. In terms of content, logical analysis, like a digital computer, can only give you back the meanings you put in it—though it may make explicit some relationship you had neglected to consider.

Postulates, then, become the roots of empirically relevant theory: in our postulates lie our articulated meanings. What

then can we say about them? To begin with, it seems evident
that they should be as inclusive as possible, so that theory is
general in the broadest sense. We do not want a theory that
deals only with the middle class family in Vienna during the
fin-de-siècle. Postulates should not be overinclusive in particulars, for articulation then becomes very difficult. We do
not want a theory about a one-eyed Jewish submarine radio
operator.

One such postulate important in contemporary sociology
can be stated as follows: Any group that is a means to an
end will, over time, become in some degree an end in itself.
Such a proposition, growing out of the work in industrial
sociology where the primary group was "rediscovered," has
a reach as wide as the creation of groups for ends. Thus the
behavior of inmates in German concentration camps, of bank
wirers in the Hawthorne plant of Western Electric, of a
bomber crew over the English Channel, are all indicated by
this postulate.

Finally, of course, we hope that our basic postulates reflect
a basic truth about society. But of this we can never be sure
a priori; therefore, we cannot demonstrate logically their value
—only their implications.

So logic cannot "prove" or "disprove" anything about empirical fact. It can only say "If . . . (such and so) then . . .
(such and so) ." The "if" is a big one and requires empirical
knowledge—finally, sense data. In short, logic operates strictly
at the analytical level; it can help us to discover the full
meaning of our theories. Beginning with the assumption that
contradiction is not allowed, that *"X"* cannot be equal to
"not-X," it spells out the implications in a system of abstract
relationships.

It is thus the science of abstract form. It embraces mathematics as a special case, and indeed mathematics has been
derived from symbolic logic. There are many formal logics
possible and one, Aristotelian logic, held sway for many centuries. Based upon classification, rather than mathematics,
Aristotle's logic deals with discrete entities in an either–or
framework. Contemporary logic, influenced heavily by mathe-

matical modes of thought, emphasizes the variable and the continuum, "more than" and "less than," based upon a relational view of the world. It is a science of relationships.

Logical relationships are not self-evident. (If they were, we would be spared perpetrating and listening to a great deal of nonsense.) To be sure, some people have developed a better "logical head" than others; the operations of analysis we have discussed come habitually and easily to them. But formal logic can help to make these processes explicit and guard against error that is ubiquitous in the esthetic, emotional detail, the surface of experience. For logical relations are, in one sense, inevitable. Since they are, after all, simply the explication of the postulates as we have defined them, including the operating rules, they are inevitable by definition.

Empirically, they are never inevitable. In all cases they are, at best, probability statements—though the probabilities are very high in some cases. The autonomy of logic, resulting from its truth by definition, produces its empirical blindness. Its applicability to the spatio-temporal continuum is always problematic and requires that the implications of the symbolic map be explored.

THE LIMITS OF LOGICAL ARGUMENT

Logic applies to discursive reasoning, to the formulations of language (including such special languages as mathematics). But there are a great many forms of expression and communication that cannot be analyzed, criticized, or evaluated through logic. Conventionally the content of these forms is simply termed "feeling" and avoided by reasonable logicians. This rigidity, says Langer, results from "two basic assumptions [that] go hand in hand: (1) *That language is the only means of articulating thought,* and (2) That *everything which is not speakable thought, is feeling."*

To be sure, this is a surrender of a great deal of human experience to unreason. It results in a low evaluation of human discourse. In this view then Langer continues:

At best, human thought is but a tiny, grammar-bound island, in the midst of a sea of feeling expressed by "Oh-Oh" and sheer babble. The island has a periphery, perhaps, of mud—factual and hypothetical concepts broken down by the emotional tides into the "material mode," a mixture of meaning and nonsense. Most of us live the better part of our lives on this mud-flat; but in artistic moods we take to the deep, where we flounder about with symptomatic cries that sound like propositions about life and death, good and evil, substance, beauty and other non-existent topics.

Thus much of our experience is excluded from reason; interpreted as nonsense, it reflects no credit on the race.

It is more useful to remember that all experience has an esthetic component, and that we express and communicate the esthetic in forms other than those of discursive reason. The plastic arts, music, the drama, are not to be analyzed in the same semantic as discursive reason. Even though its materials are verbal, poetry is not kin to prose argument (here the conventional view is correct) but it is not nonsense (here the conventional view is nonsense.) Indeed, as poetry approaches prose argument it loses its esthetic value, as in this remarkable verse of Samuel Johnson:

> As with my hat upon my head
> I walk'd along the Strand,
> I there did meet another man
> With his hat in his hand.

But when we move away from literality, we move toward a meaning which is distinctively that of poetry:

> The left side of her world is gone—
> The rest sustained by memory
> and a realization: There are still the children.
>
> Going down our porch steps her pastor
> calls back: "We are proud of her recovery,
> And there is a chiropractor up in Galesburg. . . ."
>
> The birthdays of the old require such candles.

These lines from "Strokes" by William Stafford evoke an enormity of meaning. It is meaning analyzable neither in terms of concrete facts (we have no idea if any of this happened) nor general principles. Instead, each word and phrase must be seen within the context of the poem itself. Poetry, then, may actually change our use of the language through revealing unsuspected connotations and evocations. In this sense Shakespeare created a good part of the English language.

Such a statement as "Strokes" is not falsifiable. Neither atomic fact nor general law is relevant. And since it is not falsifiable, it cannot be true; there is no logical "truth value" for art. It cannot be proven that the Johnson poem is equal to, inferior to, or superior to Stafford's on the grounds of literal truth (indeed, Johnson is embarrassingly literal). All that we can talk about is its appropriateness, its evocation of an aspect of experience that it organizes. Art must be its own proof.

To be sure, illogic that violates the structure of the poem tends to invalidate the poetry. But note the independent criterion: the structure of the poem. Those who dismiss poetry as emotional babbling simply use logic as the independent criterion and the structure of the poem is judged, for the most part, as illogic. Thus is the fallacy of misplaced concreteness committed in the name of discursive reasoning. As usual, it results in creating doubt about the validity of both art and logic.

Underlying the poetic statement is the power of metaphor. Stating the unknown, the hitherto unsymbolized, in new combinations of the known, it evokes meanings not possible before. One might say that all of "Strokes" is a single statement, impossible to make in another form. Such a use of language occurs at all the frontiers of our vocabulary, even in the language of formal philosophy. (Thus Whitehead speaks of "Eternal Objects" having a "tolerance" for relations with other "Eternal Objects"—though tolerance is usually seen as a specifically human and social trait.) Contrariwise, Emily

Dickinson comes close to the notion of the conceptual realm
in her metaphysical verse:

> I dwell in Possibility—
> A fairer House than Prose—
> More numerous of Windows—
> Superior—of doors—

The metaphor allows us to articulate aspects of experience
for which we have no word.

But the metaphor can become a word. It can change in
usage, from metaphorical tag to cliché to denotative language. Thus we move from the poetic statement, "All the
world's a stage," to the notions of "role theory" in social
science. When we combine another flattened metaphor, the
notion of "stress and strain" transferred from physical objects
to the perturbation of human psyches, we come out with
studies of "Stress in the Role of Foreman."

For the postulates underlying scientific theory quite often
have origins in metaphors. New postulates are frequently
necessarily metaphorical, in origin and form, as they are
efforts to name an unknown aspect of experience. Yet in the
process of metaphorical thinking the origins of poetry and
the origins of scientific theory seem strangely close together.
For this reason some have argued that the metaphor, the
analogical factor, is the most powerful engine of the human
mind, the origin of meaning.

Both uses of metaphor, the poetic and the scientific, are
notably nonhistorical. The actual course of events in the
world, recorded in their detail, is used as materials for the
creation of an ahistorical social science, a poetry which evokes
and celebrates certain creative responses of men to the course
of events. The scientist, or the poet, brings the raw materials
of history into his laboratory and *creates* physical nature, or
esthetic value. In the process the operation with and upon
concepts through a set of logical rules is critical for the
scientist (though he may use mathematics and forget its
logical base); the rules for the poet are otherwise.

The poet evokes a possible order for experience. But its adequacy varies with the ethos of the reader, and that is why we cannot obtain universal agreement on the value of his artifact. We cannot measure the response of the observer (and, as we will see later, measurement is critical for science). Since this is so, our terms have meanings that shift from subject to subject, and do not allow the use of the negative: we cannot disprove value.

If we have standardized our ethos we can agree, of course, to like and dislike the same things. Such agreement may seem like "intersubjective validity" in science—until we confront those who differ.

[9]

MATHEMATICS:
A SPECIAL LOGICAL LANGUAGE

Mathematics has been called "the most original creation of the human spirit." It departs furthest from nature and our naive experience of it; its forms are not given in our conceptualization of sense data. There is nothing about an object that would lead us to multiply its dimensions by themselves, to square and to cube; nothing in nature resembles the square root. Then when we reach unreal numbers, the square root of minus 1, we are indeed in fairyland. It seems to be a form of conceptual play, a fantasy of the logical intellect.

Yet this play produces a complete abstract generality, a language for all occasions. It is a language which crosses the boundaries of human groups, which holds true without respect to environment. It is a form of logic and, like all logic, analytical—but it is the purest and highest technique of analysis. The explication of its postulates has created the most complex symbolic structure we have thus far imagined. It is serious play, with limiting rules and a rigorous constraint.

The beginning was the discovery of number. This was the discovery of a useful analogy between groups of things, whatever their nature; that groups of loaves and fishes and apples and worms may be matched against each other member by member, and be in one sense identical. It was a great achievement thus to abstract similarity that completely avoids any implication as to the nature of the specific object save its existence, its capacity to have a number stand for it.

In number is the source of arithmetic. One can perform

operations with numbers that are cumbersome or impossible with real objects, yet the world of real objects will correspond with these operations. (There have been ingenious efforts to approximate number. In the census in Dahomey, each member of a village was represented by one pebble placed in a basket; the baskets were then compared by level. A quasi number system emerged. Dahomean society was a complexly developed world, yet number had only a limited development.) Arithmetic, the study of numbers, is the first creation of pure mathematics.

Algebra developed by analogy. Instead of saying "Take five (of anything)" the algebraicist said, in effect, "Take any number." Thus the origin of the variable, a term that can be of any magnitude in a given mathematical argument. But as abstraction went on its merry course, it moved beyond the variable to the function: "Take any function"—that is, function as the relationship of variables. And analysis was further strengthened by the inclusion of the spatialized mathematics, geometry and trigonometry; their propositions (say, the relations among angles and sides in triangles) could be summarized in terms of functions and included in more general propositions. In summary, according to Whitehead, the discovery of mathematics was the discovery "that the totality of those general abstract conditions, which are concurrently applicable to the relationships among the entities of any one concrete occasion, are in *themselves interconnected* in the manner of a pattern with a key to it. . . ."

Thus any given number may be a part of an equation that is describable by a mathematical function and can be related to others. Number exists in an infinite setting, mathematics is a seamless web. But what is the "key"?

From a select set of those general conditions, exemplified in one and the same occasion, a pattern involving an infinite variety of other such conditions, also exemplified in the same occasion, *can be developed by the pure exercise of abstract logic* . . . Any such select set is called the set of *postulates,* or *premises* from which the reasoning proceeds . . . this reasoning is the exhibition of the whole pattern of general conditions involved in the pattern derived from the postulates.

Mathematics is then a logic, a creation of the human mind of the utmost abstraction, for it deals with the most abstract unit—number. Like any logic, it is the articulation of the implications in the postulates. And in the postulates lie the rules for the rigorous game. All were created by man.

But much of this creation has been found to "work," its patterns corresponding to the structure of things. This is to me amazing, a miracle often hidden by our tacit acceptance of the creations of science. For some reason, the force exerted on Galileo's "body" is related to its mass and acceleration by multiplication, one of the simplest kinds of numerical transformation. Out of such coincidence developed the enormous achievements of physical science. Number was applied to measurable aspects of commonplace, everyday experience; those numbered aspects were then related by mathematical operations, and the results predicted new and hitherto unknown relationships in that experienced world.

The tremendous utility of mathematics as a conceptual tool in physical science has encouraged its application in the social sciences. It is well to note, however, Whitehead's cautionary words on the application of mathematics to other aspects of experience.

It often happens, therefore, that in criticizing a learned book of applied mathematics . . . one's whole trouble is with the first chapter, or even with the first page. For it is there, at the very outset, where the author will probably be found to slip in his assumptions. Farther, the trouble is not with what the author does say, but with what he does not say. Also it is not with what he knows he has assumed, but with what he has unconsciously assumed. We do not doubt the author's honesty. It is his perspicacity which we are criticizing.

Thus in the application of mathematics to a problem we must be certain that the mathematical conditions hold, and to do this they must be all specified (and not include unnecessary conditions). These assumptions include such things as, in statistics, a random sample, a continuous variable, and a "normal curve" distribution for certain kinds of reasoning. If these conditions are not satisfied they may easily turn our work into a parody of reasoning, a "Potemkin Village" of precision, a mock-up to hide rather than reveal reality.

There is, further, the problem of relating the mathematical formulations to the conceptual realm. We shall discuss this further in considering problems of measurement; let us simply note how great the leap from a concept, however abstract in the interpretative sense, to a mathematical formulation. After we make this leap, however, we have substituted the mathematical form—and anything we have left out cannot to put back in. Whitehead again: "If anything out of relationship, then complete ignorance as to it. Here by 'ignorance,' I mean *ignorance;* accordingly no advice can be given as to how to expect it, or to treat it, in 'practice' or in any other way." The price of interpretative abstraction and mathematization alike is to leave out aspects of thought.

Finally we must be sure that the particular instance we are studying is a good sample of other instances. This will be more difficult as there is more variability in the phenomena under consideration. In social science the sampling problem is critical: if we wish to study "the American family" we had better protect ourselves with a representative sample, for kinship structure varies greatly, from that of Negroes in the Yazoo delta to the forms occurring in Park Avenue penthouses. In general, the size of the sample should increase with the heterogeneity of the population it comes from. Thus the anthropologist may settle for a smaller sample if "his tribe" is homogeneous with respect to what he is interested in. (But then, he needs an independent proof of that regularity, for a small sample will not tell him.)

We always return to the nature of the event that is problematic. This determines, finally, the kind of general propositions we can make; thus the units which we conceptualize in our experience of nature have a rigor as constraining as that of the mathematical realm. We must always ask three kinds of questions: What aspects of our subject are quantifiable, measurable in terms of real number? And: What existing mathematics will apply to them? Finally: How appropriate are the mathematics we use to the nature of our hypotheses?

TYPES OF SPACES

The mathematics we use was developed to treat, first physical space (in geometry, measurement of the earth) and later the physics of simple location. It is notable that some of the great advances in mathematics were created by the same physicists who applied them: they were tools for given jobs. Arthur Bentley has raised the question: Are these the most appropriate tools for the spaces that social scientists must study? In answering it, he discusses five kinds of space.

1. *Vulgar space:* "any system of space which is expressed and accepted by the people of any specific social time and social place as "external" to them, and as the physical locus in which they find themselves; and which is embodied in their current meanings of pertinent words, and taken in account in their own understanding of their own practical life."

2. *Mathematical space:* "the various constructions in full symbolic form which mathematicians have developed, beginning historically with Euclidian space . . ."

3. *Physical space:* "those mathematical spaces which at any given social time and place are taken by physicists as best organizing the results of physical and astronomical observation and experiment."

4. *Social space:* "those discretenesses and continuities, those separations and distributions and purely social mensurations, which are found among men outspread in societies."

5. *Sociological space:* "theoretical constructions which, with respect to social spaces, hold a position comparable to that of mathematical spaces with respect to physical science."

Bentley notes that physical and mathematical spaces are created by society, an aspect of knowledge, while the society is itself affected by these creations. Thus Euclidean space reflected and reinforced the Greek view that objects are preeminent, with "space" merely the relations between them; Newton made of space a "thing"; relativity leaves us with a difficult world of space–time, of relative position.

The implications for social science are clear. Both Newtonian space and clock time are simply among the alternatives available for the construction of spaces most appropriate to the study of society. There is nothing inherent in statute miles that is necessarily meaningful for social interaction. And indeed, sociologists have invented the concept of the "space–time" ratio to indicate that the social meaning of space (whether as separator or channel of interaction) must always be considered in terms of the cost of movement—in time and other values. This "interactional space," as the planner John Friedman calls it, is the only space relevant for many problems. The topography of interactional space does not usually resemble that of the geographers. It identifies barriers to movement (political boundaries, ethnic boundaries) and vectors of movement for men, materials, and messages (access to different forms of transport and communications media). In short, a reconsideration of space in its social meanings lets us make it *internal* to concepts dealing with the reality of social structure.

This view is not based only upon contemporary society. Many primitive peoples have measured distance by time; the number of "moons" that will occur during a journey may be an adequate approximation of the distance—perhaps it is the only significant aspect of distance for the given culture group. This leads us to emphasize the *dimensions* that are relevant for social scientific problems. In Bentley's words, "What the social dimensions are, or more properly, what the most important social dimensions are for any specialized line of investigation, is our sociological problem in general. The search for precision in their analysis and use is the sociological space problem in general. The search for precision in their analysis and use is the sociological space problem." With the development of dimensions, "systems of coordinates may be aimed at in social spaces with exactly the meaning they have in mathematics."

The most general term for sociological coordinates is what Lazarsfeld and Barton call "attribute space." This space locates units *vis-à-vis* each other along various dimensions

important to theoretical analysis, and *only* on such dimensions.

A CASE IN POINT

Given some six million people scattered over the 2,500 square miles of the Los Angeles metropolitan area, and given thirty items of information on each household, the problem is how best to order this information for sociological analysis. One solution to this problem exemplifies some of the argument of this chapter.

One could organize the distribution of given attributes (size of family, color, nationality background, age, education) on the map, using small subunits called census tracts. You would have for each neighborhood a set of measures for each item; you could summarize them with an average or median for convenience. But such an approach tends to submerge whatever order exists in a sea of detail. The geographical map is, after all, merely a container for the data; it tells us of propinquity in Newtonian space and little else.

One solution was developed by Shevky and his associates. Beginning with some theoretically important dimensions, social rank, ethnicity, and lifestyle, they constructed indexes for each of these using data collected by the census. These indexes, using only a few measures, turned out to be so highly correlated with all the other census information that they could be said to summarize them (see chapter 1, pp. 15–16). As the next step, the indexes were used to construct an attribute space having three dimensions. In the figure on p. 102 the division of the attribute space was as follows. The horizontal field was divided into *thirds of the range*. The vertical field was divided by the regression of urbanization on social rank, with one standard deviation from the mean defining the middle tier of areas (II, V, VIII). Later, it became clear that the correlation between urbanization and social rank was negligible (.17); at this time it seemed appropriate to use an

arbitrary cutting point; i.e., quartiles on the range by urbanization and social rank. (See Shevky and Bell's *Social Area
Analysis*.)

SOCIAL AREA ATTRIBUTE SPACE

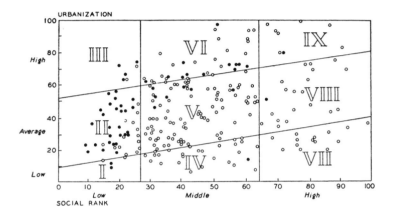

Census Tracts: o=Less ethnic than average
● =More ethnic than average

The Social Areas of the San Francisco Bay Region

We are now able to see the similarity and dissimilarity among
the hundreds of census tract populations simultaneously.
Their distance in the constructed space refers precisely to their
difference along these three dimensions.

We can now go back to the metaphor of the map, if we
choose. In doing so we would identify by symbol the relative
social nature of each geographical subunit. This would be
well worth doing if our aim were to study the relations between, say, propinquity and social characteristics. (Indeed,
one study indicated that informal visiting tended to be with
people living in neighborhoods of the same social rank, ethnicity, and life style, i.e., propinquity in social rather than

physical space. And when people indicated they would like to move, it was to neighborhoods of similar life style and higher social rank, whether or not in the same geographical region of the city.)

But we can gain great freedom for other kinds of analysis by continuing to use the attribute space. The position of a census tract in the coordinates may be more important than its position within the layout of the metropolis. We may, for example, be interested in relations among the dimensions: Are lifestyle and social rank correlated? (They are, but the coefficient is low.) Are the distributions of tracts continuous along each dimension, or do we have clusters and gaps? And using political space, where in attribute space are the Central City neighborhoods, Gold Coast, and Ghetto, compared with suburban neighborhoods?

Further, by locating the metropolis as a galaxy of neighborhoods in attribute space, one has an efficient means for comparing different cities. The entire configuration of the cities may be compared, and correlated with such matters as age in historical time, technological time (they are not the same), economic base, or region of the nation.

Finally, attribute space implies correlational analysis. Thus the spread distributions may always be transformed into linear statements, equations which yield further information. We can compare, for example, voting in different sorts of neighborhoods. Using the three dimensions indicated above and their theoretical relevance for political behavior, we can see how well they predict the proportion who vote and the direction of their vote. (In some studies they predicted very well indeed, accounting for around 70 per cent of the variation from neighborhood to neighborhood.) In short, we can take discrete data, organize it by a constructed space, and transform the space back to nonspatial statements.

The critical thing is the kind of space we use to organize data. It should be isomorphic with the interactions of the kinds of units our theory is about. Thus the criticism of human ecology that emphasizes its dealing with residential neighborhoods while much of our most important behavior occurs outside them is simply an indication of one limit to the kind of attribute space analyzed above. An attribute space can as easily be constructed for "men working" or "men praying." The critical thing is the aspect of social life to be abstracted, examined, and related to other aspects through observation and interpretation. The geographical map is a metaphor; many others will do as well or better.

A RECAPITULATION

Logic is a way of analyzing abstract form. Taking arguments from the conceptual realm, it spells out the meaning of the propositions. Mathematics is a way of creating abstract forms based upon number. Both have a very problematic relation to the spatio-temporal continuum, the experienced world. Logical proof may be quite independent of empirical proof, for the latter demands the validity of basic assumptions (or in logic, postulates). Mathematical reasoning may or may not have any relevance to the structures adduced from empirical research.

The problem in social science is to create abstract forms, having an orderly and determinate relationship among themselves, corresponding to the forms encountered in social experience. One may, however, use the relations of abstract form to speculate about the relations of empirical form. Thus in statistics we consider the normal or "bell shaped" curve, a geometrical form about which a great deal can be said *on purely logical grounds*. We apply it to the distribution of social attributes, or social behaviors, because these frequently can be rather accurately described in this fashion, with most cases piling up at the average, and a declining proportion occurring as we move away from the average in either direction, along a single dimension. For example, the Intelligence Quotient is just such a use of this mathematical artifact. We can relate this distribution (IQ) to the distribution of such behaviors as achievement in mathematics or athletics, or other activities that can be described with the same form: the result

may be a correlation coefficient (a two-dimensional statement) which shows relations that may be predictive of new
cases or other kinds of behavior.

We may also use the form of a distribution as an indicator
of social structure. Thus the normal curve may be replaced
by the "J-curve"—in a certain scene of social action. When
this happens we suspect that a social rule has been applied to
prevent some kinds of behavior—stopping at an unmarked
intersection (the normal curve) as against stopping at a boule-
vard stop sign (the J-curve). Or we may discover a distribution which is not shaped at all like a bell, but rather like a
"U."

J-Curve   Normal Curve   U-Curve

Perhaps these are attitudes toward property rights versus human rights; in this event we would suspect that we had two
different populations in the same sample or universe. Those
on the right might be employers, those on the left, employees.

In short, we use abstract forms however derived because we
suspect they have important implications for empirical events
we observe. In the physical sciences the use of mathematical
form has had the most spectacular success of this kind. But it
is important to remember that mathematical formulation of
a theory is no guarantee whatsoever of its validity. The mathematics may be perfectly correct, the logical argument im-
pregnable, and both quite irrelevant to the scientific problem.

If we are lucky, however, and find a correspondence between forms, then we can move rapidly. Finding the necessary abstract form one can put in his assumptions as the
postulates and deduce other expected relationships—those
which will hold if the abstract form is indeed isometric with

the order of facts. One notes the datum, relates it to the conceptual structure where it is in orderly relation to other concepts, and saying "If . . . then . . . ," expects to find other data related to his clue in the expected fashion. If this is so, he has found a "hanging together" in the structure of things corresponding to the order of his theory: the map is isometric with the landscape, the landscape ordered by the map.

[III]

A WORKING DEFINITION

[10]

THEORY, LAW, AND TEST

The social enterprise called science inherited from the prescientific Christian world view a faith in lawful order. But order of what? We have already noted that it cannot be exclusive to the world out there nor can it be exclusive to our inner psychological field. Perhaps the best statement of the mission is Norman Campbell's, "Science is the study of *those judgments* concerning which universal agreement can be obtained." Such a ground for the value of science is sometimes called "intersubjective validity," the first term indicating agreement, the second fidelity to experience.

Thus the events relevant to science are those accessible to the judgment of all interested men. The scientist cannot study the cosmology experienced by a person suffering hallucinations (as cosmology) but he can study mirages. When in Maryland a dozen unacquainted persons see, independently, a white domed city corresponding to Dakar, in Africa (where none of them has ever been), we have an example of intersubjective validity, however strange. (What it means in terms of optics is, of course, another matter.) The important thing is that the occurrence was not wholly private; there was an event outside the individual nervous system.

But there are difficulties. What of those with deviant nervous systems—the blind, the deaf, or even the color-blind, the tone-deaf? In practice, we postulate "standard men" for whom judgment is possible among the complex of recurrent events and among whom there can be agreement. But the standard man is an assumption, a hypothesis to be tested. There is always the possibility of error in our estimates; sensitivity may vary enormously, new senses may emerge. (Nobody has demonstrated that the process of evolution, a major aspect of the past, has come to a halt in the present.)

In dealing with deviant cases of observation and therefore judgment, we are forced to complicate the notion of standard man. "The observer" is always an individual, conceptualizing person. Thus we must keep in mind the observer himself as an object of study and, in that role, his "personality"—not as an ineffable and unique organism, but as a cluster of "impersonal" variables including variations in sensitivity. Thus far we have in the physical sciences been able to "control" for individual differences, reaching agreement through acknowledging them and their effects upon observation. This control is made easier by the recurrence of the events studied and the relative ease of bringing them about in the laboratory.

In social science agreement is much more difficult. Some have argued that this problem is inherent in the observer-event relationship since there is, first, enormous variation in the way men perceive social events and, second, enormous volatility and variation in the events perceived. Thus they argue that we are subject to gross error multiplied by gross error, the result a near madhouse.

This argument ignores several important circumstances. First, communication tends to force agreement through the emergence of general concepts; those concepts tend to standardize men—and even their senses. Second, there are enormous regularities in human life, as well as a volatile and various surface; too often we confuse the esthetics of the surface with the regularities of association. While the firestorms vary on the suns, regularities in the relationship of heat, wind currents, and the like remain intact; while the nature of childhood varies fantastically around the globe, the invariant relation between survival of the newborn child and (some) adult sponsorship remains intact. Our abstraction of relevant aspects often does not go far enough, nor deep enough.

Yet there are limits. We have seen that there are many events that are simply nonsharable experiences of the actor (though crude approximations may be attempted, a facsimile created for discourse that may be useful). And then there is that private knowledge in principle sharable but because it occurred only once, in privacy, never really sharable. A tree falls in the forest, a book in a room. Are such events subject to scientific knowledge?

Not in themselves. But then, every particular event is excluded from scientific inquiry; this is the distinction between science and history. The latter is usually obsessed with the particular, the former concerned only in a very limited way. In scientific inquiry we are interested in abstracted aspects of existing or possible classes of repetitive events, and we are interested in the given event only as it relates to other events. Science is the study of relationships. So in summary: the scientist is interested in "judgments of relations between classes of events, concerning which universal agreement can be obtained."

LAWS AND KINDS OF LAWS

There are two kinds of proposition upon which there can be universal agreement: logical propositions and empirical propositions. The former we have already dealt with; their validity is given in their definitions, the assumptions require the conclusions because they are implicit. The Cheshire cat grins because that grin is included in the definition of the Cheshire cat.

The empirical propositions are of two sorts. One we may call "descriptive laws," the other "relational laws." Descriptive laws are no less than the definitions of events that constitute the facts in a situation. Universal agreement must begin with this kind of law, and from it derive the units of inquiry. They usually amount to complex concepts, abstractive hierarchies in which a number of attributes are involved in the same event. They are the "things" we study as stones, plants, animals, men.

Descriptive laws come out of the folk culture, out of the common-sense interpretations of the world around, created and conserved in the cultural vocabulary. Because for hundreds of thousands of years men had discriminated among their sense impressions, had noticed coherences which repeated, had *named* them, the basic units were present for the development of science. There were immense and detailed "folk zoologies," "folk botanies," and their interactions— "folk medicines," long before the development of sophisticated life sciences. It was with this Noah's Ark of specimens that the latter began. Some folk units are simple, but most are combinations of great complexity, reflecting accumulated knowledge (and speculation and myth) about the beast in question.

It is noteworthy that we continue to acquire descriptive laws each time a significantly new unit is discovered. Thus in the life sciences men are still busy describing the denizens of earth, and may have their chance on other planets. At the same time, we are creating as well as discovering: sometimes in direct consequence of understanding the structures that exist, more often with some knowledge, experimentally. We alter matter into "rare earths," we create "isotopes," we produce new breeds of plant and animal. Be it noted also that in our social media we continue to create, discover, and then name what occurs: the nation state, the bureaucracy, the labor union, the corporation. We will continue to create new forms, in part through understanding the basic variables underlying these.

Out of the descriptive laws and the resulting units derive the first concerns of social science. "What do we mean by social?" is more often mooted than answered. At the broadest level one can speak of the mutual modification of action among living things; this is the ecologist's position. Or one can limit it to the interaction among animals, or among men. But if the latter is accepted as a definition, we must then ask: What is man? How human is the paretic, with most of his brain tissue gone, incapable of responding? How human the isolated child studied by Kingsley Davis, who had never learned speech, walked upright, seen the world? (To be sure, she was capable of learning; the paretic does not have even this.)

There are two common solutions to the problem of the unit for inquiry. One is to begin with the animal form, a descriptive law similar to that of the bobcat or elephant, and to make the actions problematic—let them act as they must act. Another solution is to focus on the unit of interaction and judge the specifically "human" and "social" by the prescribed nature of that interaction. This is a much more difficult approach, for it requires a rather fully developed theory of human interaction before one can isolate such an event. The former, essentially a folk definition, is probably most commonly accepted in the practical work of social science as well as in our common-sense discourse. Much of the interesting "metatheoretical" controversy in social science centers around this problem of defining the units; we will discuss it in more detail later (Chapter 13).

Investigation beginning with the descriptive laws, the culturally given, then proceeds in two directions. In one, it relates the object, defined by the culture as a complex concept referring to a set of invariant attributes, to other objects. Thus we move up to larger complexes. These are sometimes called *molar* laws of relationship—the cannon ball and its trajectory through space, its career down the inclined plane. We can also move downward, separating the object into component parts in terms of our frame of reference; thus the structure of the cannon ball may be our focus. The results of this latter are sometimes called *molecular* laws of relationship. It is obvious that whether a given law is molar or molecular depends upon one's focus of attention (the atomic structure underlying the molecular is "still more molecular"—while the molecular is molar to the atomic analysis). In the study of human behavior, personality is sometimes considered molecular, society molar.

The notion of relational laws between molar objects often means that we accept the objects as given by the folk culture. We look for relations between relations, between cannon

ball and plane. But as our relational laws become more precise we lose, in the given case, detail that is irrelevant to the
laws we create. Thus we redefine, from "cannon ball" to
"round object of given mass." Our structure of laws grows
more complex, however, and also more abstract (in both
senses of the term): we now deal with moving objects, angles
of planes, attraction of another mass—the earth. We move
to a broader *synthesis* of laws about narrowly abstracted aspects of the "things" with which we started.

On the other hand, we move downward through analysis.
Here we both discriminate among the class of things we first
addressed and analyze the structure of each. The cannon ball
may be seen as a community of molecules, the social group as a
community of role players. And discriminating among the
class of objects, we may compare structures and exercise a
finer definition, creating subclasses. Thus the variations in
molecular structure of cannon balls with similar mass but
varying alloys, the variations in role systems among groups
having the same folk designation (the foreman-dominated
work group, as compared to a work group controlled by an
oligarchy of the older members).

While in molar analysis we take the folk definition as given
for our purpose, we take it only provisionally. We transform it
by abstracting some attributes (shape, mass) and disregarding
others. In molecular analysis we transform the folk definition, the original descriptive law, by showing another nature
of the object; we may greatly weaken its original significance
by showing the crudeness of folk categories. Such a concept as
that of rural–urban social differences may become trivial when
we note the variations within both rural and urban society
and the overall similarity of the two, as in such contemporary
societies as the U. S. and Canada. In the process of analysis
we move to new descriptive laws. for folk thought is too crude
for accuracy.

As an example of such analysis, let us take the study of
deviation and control in social science. Beginning with the
folk definition, the descriptive law, crime is an act against
formal law and the criminal the perpetrator of that act. But

as shown by Edwin Lemert, upon which work I will draw
extensively in this example, if we use available data and
estimates it seems likely that the criminal population is a
majority of the population in the United States under the
common-sense definition of crime.

There are a number of common-sense ways of classifying
criminals. One is by the nature of the crime, one is by
"habitual" as against occasional, one by participation in organized as against unorganized crime. Looking at the invariants, however, Lemert noted three quite different processes
resulting in deviant acts defined as criminal. First, there are
many crimes committed by people responding to a radical
change in the situation: in the case of revolution where a
country is evenly divided pro and con, who is criminal in
breaking the existing laws? The winners usually decide. (The
Nuremberg trials were another version of this: Who is a war
criminal?) At a more pedestrian level, people who smoked
marijuana in the early years of this century were law abiding
but, after passage of laws against the practice, they suddenly
became criminals.

Other crimes are committed as a result of deep-seated personality dynamics. (Jack the Ripper or the Boston Strangler
are such.) Lemert, as a sociologist, does not study these—he
merely notes that some acts classified as criminal result from
psychopathic processes.

Finally, he notes that some deviation is systematic. That is,
deviation has become a part of the person's ordinary, everyday style of life. He speaks of the professional criminal, the
prostitute, the narcotics addict, and others as manifesting
such "systematic deviation." They are not necessarily psychologically atypical, and their deviation is not the result of the
larger situation and its abrupt changes. Their self-concept,
their view of themselves, is as "deviants" in the given fashion.

This analysis radically shifts the meaning of the terms
"crime" and "criminal." In practice, neither refers to a uniform, meaningful class of things. Both the process producing
the criminal act, and the kind of social policy that would
prevent it, are obviously different for each of the three classes

of deviants. Systematic, repetitive deviation is the most interesting from Lemert's point of view; disregarding the psychological deviant, he then considers the systematic deviant.

Here his analysis is molar. He notes that most people perform illegal acts at some time during their lives; with apprehension they are literally felons or misdemeanants. But the
systematic deviants repeat. His theory of the systematic criminal traces the repetition of deviation to the consequences of
the earliest deviation. The argument goes: After the apprehension, the societal response to the person is such as to
encourage a change in his own definition of himself. He sees
himself as others see him; no longer a high school student, he
is now a "juvenile delinquent," a criminal. As this occurs,
the society around also redefines him and the result is a narrowing of his social opportunities, accompanied by rewards
for continuing his deviation. When he reaches the point
where in response to his situation as a "defined deviant" he
repeats the original deviation (further narrowing his alternatives), he has become a systematic deviant. In parallel fashion, one becomes addicted to narcotics only if he knows what
is troubling him and knows that further use of narcotics will
dissipate the pains of "withdrawal." In short, Lemert spells
out a process in which consequences of action produce repetition of action—a vicious circle. Much of what we call social
structure may well be seen as a similar kind of circle, with
deviation subsumed as a special case.

We should note the interaction of molar and molecular
anaylsis. Molecular analysis allows us to abstract meaningful
aspects out of the complex whole, "crime" and "criminals,"
while molar analysis allows us to relate the criminal role to
role theory in general—the responding self, the societal response, the self image. In practice, we use both sorts of analysis all the time, thus transforming our conceptual vocabulary,
creating new laws of description and relationship. To repeat,
there are no Laws in nature, although nature accepts some of
the laws that we create.

THE PERMANENCE OF LAWS

But why do we believe that the laws we have discovered will hold true in the future? How do we generalize? This is the essential problem of induction, as ordinarily conceived; it is, in Whitehead's words, "the despair of philosophy." We see how the syllogism works: All men are fools; Socrates is a man; therefore Socrates is a fool. But the deductive reasoning is not reversible. We cannot say: Socrates is a man; Socrates is a fool; therefore all men are fools. In the same case, we cannot say: In our sample X and Y are invariably associated, therefore in all future cases of X there will be Y. Yet the deduction that allows us to understand a given case finally depends upon the induction that goes from particular to general. And that induction is faulty, both logically and empirically.

Yet we have said laws are invariant associations. We obviously must limit that definition. One way to do this is simply to say: Laws describe what has already occurred; they indicate the patterns in past experience with great fidelity. When I predict about things not yet known, it is a different order of statement. It is shorthand for something like this: *If* the universe (including man) retains its past habits precisely, *then* my descriptions of the past will also apply to the new present that will occur, if I correctly identify that present.

And the universe does retain those habits. Just why laws based on past samples should continue to work, we cannot say. Campbell is eloquent: "The final answer that I must give is that I do not know, that nobody knows, and that probably nobody ever will know. The position is simply this . . ." It is paradoxical that the immense order we see in the world is at the same time the most gigantic example of arbitrariness. It need not have been so.

In practice we survey our past experience (nobody can survey future experience) and construct statements of regularity that correspond to aspects of it. We then gather new data, new experiences of the same kind of event, to see if it fits these regularities, these provisional laws we have created.

By reiteration we test repetitiveness. If we are ingenious, we create new but comparable events for our use—we experiment. And because of our control of the circumstances of that event, we may be able to vary significant aspects of it to make our laws more specific, and therefore sensitive to variation.

If the new data do not fit our laws, what then? We can, of course, simply discard the law—and sometimes that is clearly necessary. If one believes, on deductive grounds, that women have more teeth than men, and specimen after specimen has about the same number, the law doesn't help and is discarded. More common, however, is a strategy called "deviant case analysis." Every case that does not fit the law is examined rigorously. The deviant case may simply turn out to be a mistake (it was not really a woman) ; such inquiry may force us to improve our descriptive law, the law which led us to choose the case in the first place. But should the descriptive law be adequately specified, we are then forced to modify our relational law. It will probably now stand: If this, then that, *under certain conditions.* Laws stated with the clause "all other things being equal" are at the mercy of those other things, and they are usually discovered only through empirical research. Their discovery may greatly limit the generality of the law.

Donald Cressey's study of the "embezzler syndrome" illuminates these considerations. Embezzlers, people who use their official position to steal from their employers, are atypical criminals: they are better educated than the average citizen, usually have no past criminal record, and are respectable. They are typically auditors, accountants, executive officers of banks or churches—highly respected, solid citizens. Existing data also indicate that a large proportion of them have been involved in gambling, extramarital sex relations, or some other form of "riotous living" before their apprehension.

Cressey's first interpretation followed the lines of Sutherland's theory (see chapter 3). It will be remembered that Sutherland believed a man becomes criminal as he associates more intensely with criminals than noncriminals (thus learning the techniques and norms of criminality) and as he has the opportunity for pursuing the role. But when Cressey interviewed a sample of embezzlers he discovered the theory did not apply. These men had no history of past association with embezzlers. Further, they did not need to learn techniques for embezzling: anyone who knows how to operate as an accountant also knows how to falsify records. (Indeed, detecting embezzlers is part of the course of instruction at accounting schools.) Thus the solitary embezzler was a puzzle in Sutherland's framework.

Cressey saw embezzling as a breakdown in the role definition of the actor. Using past data on embezzlers as clues, he considered both the incidence of riotous living at the time of the crime and the "white collar" status, the respectability of the criminals, and he concluded that such people would not, because of this status, be able to seek help if they got in trouble about their riotous living. They could not confess the behavior. Therefore the "nonsharable problem" was the critical precipitate of embezzling. But these are obvious deviant cases: most of us have nonsharable problems, but few of us embezzle. Thus he added the qualifier, a "nonsharable problem which can be solved by financial means."

He applied this proposition to a large sample of convicted embezzlers, with generally confirming results, but, again, negative cases. There were embezzlers who had no such problems; and there were people with the opportunity for embezzlement who had acted otherwise. This finding led him to further specify his descriptive laws: those who had no such problem turned out to be people who had deliberately taken the position as accountant with the intention of robbing the organization. By law they were embezzlers, but by Cressey's standards they were merely ingenious thieves. So he added to the definition of embezzlers as those who steal from their employers the proviso "after taking a position of financial trust in good faith." In short, the crime had to follow ordinary job performance and intention. This new definition had the effect of clarifying the nature of the behavior and eliminating a sample of a quite different criminal population. As for those who did not em-

bezzle, he was forced to reinterview his sample of embezzlers
for clues. In the process he found that each of them recalled
a period in which he persuaded himself that the act was not
criminal, he would return the money, it was a loan. This
rationalization, which allowed the criminal act without a
moral conflict, made crime possible for these ordinarily conformist individuals.

Thus Cressey was in a position to propose as follows: embezzlers are individuals who have violated a position of financial trust after taking it in good faith. They are individuals
who have incurred a nonsharable problem which is financially
solvable; they have the objective opportunity to perform
the criminal act and, through rationalization (or symbolic
redefinition) of the act, the subjective opportunity. He found
this to hold for each of some two hundred cases of embezzlers whom he studied. His laws described his population.

But there is another question we must raise. Are all people
who have these attributes (a nonsharable problem of a given
nature, opportunity, and rationalization) also embezzlers?
About this Cressey can say nothing on the basis of his studies.
He can say that he formulated laws that relate a given act
performed by many men to a natural process which, in every
case, included the conditions he specified. He found invariant
associations which led him to say: All embezzlers are such and
so. It could not let him say: All such and so are embezzlers.

Some argue for the permanence of laws by invoking a universal and inevitable causality. Our very term for answering
the question "Why?" implies casuality—"Because." Yet it will
be remembered that there is really no "why" for the structure
of experience, merely a description of the way it happens.
Thus in the studies of déviation discussed above, there is
nothing said about causality; there is an effort to indicate invariant associations of variables.

Indeed, in scientific theory there is really no need for the
concept of causation. It is an esthetic dimension added for
esthetic reasons. In operations, causality turns out to be invariant associations in time and space. Most logical analyses of
causality insist on invariant association in time—sequence.

But relationships can frequently be specified as invariant with no attention to sequence: Which comes first, the circulation system or that state of irritability and mobility we call animal life? The question is meaningless. The statement of scientific laws does not include or require causality; it simply requires statements of invariant association in given orders.

It is likely that our esthetic need to imply causality arises from several sources. Certainly we can confuse the process of inquiry with what is found; the "classical" experimental design rests upon varying the state of an object over time. Thus we have the situation before treatment, the nature of treatment, and the resulting situation. But when we formulate a law it will not necessarily speak of time at all—it will describe relations and relations among relations. Another source of our need for cause, perhaps more important, lies in our concern for the way we use scientific law to intervene in the ongoing structure of the world. In brief, we want to know how, through controlling X, we can control Y. Yet clearly, X may simply be part of Y, the tail by which we pull the dog; our own use of knowledge is the only cause involved.

More important than "causality" for purposes of inquiry is a view of the world as natural processes, of systems and between systems, accessible to us. We can look for those processes through identifying invariant sequences in time or space. One may call the first "cause" if he likes, the latter "structure." It matters little in the enterprise of creating scientific laws: the chief value of causality is probably as a work norm inciting us to more precise formulations, more testable propositions. But naïvely applied, it may confuse discourse and leave us searching for imaginary entities.

THEORY AND LAW

We have been discussing laws, those invariant associations among observations on which it is possible to get universal agreement. However important these are, they are not enough for scientific explanation, for laws do not explain: they merely state relationships among observables. Without theory they are incomplete, mere "empirical laws." We have such laws as that of "intervening opportunity," which describes with considerable accuracy the distance migrating populations will move from a given center of settlement (it is proportionate to distance over social space). Such laws are puzzles for theory, but they are not theory.

They are adequate for prediction and in this sense laws are not unlike recipes. They may give us indexes which we can use as signs of probable correlates. But even their predictive value is limited, for without theory it is difficult to know if all relevant variables have been considered. Thus in predicting population, demographers during the 1930's made a number of predictions about the future population of the United States. Noting the correlations between urbanization, industrialization, and wealth on one hand, and a declining fertility on the other, they predicted a gradual slowdown of the American rate of increase, to the final result of a stable or even declining population. Publicists cited the demography of ancient Rome, decline and fall because of the sin of tampering with holy organisms. Yet with the end of the Depression and World War II, the United States again became one of the more fertile societies on earth. Simple extrapolation, which laws alone may tempt us to do, is a dangerous mode of prophecy.

In explanation laws do have a subsidiary value. Laws can place an event in a more general context; they can define it as a specific example of a more general regularity. But if that general regularity is simply a more general law, we must immediately ask once more for an explanation. It is in this sense that theory explains law, and explanation without theory is incomplete.

Durkheim in his research on suicide found many gross regularities. He found, for example, that suicide rates are correlated with economic depression—a relational law. They are also correlated with rapid economic growth and increasing wealth in the society. He subsumed both laws under the more general proposition: suicides increase with rapid economic change in the society. But this is no explanation. Why should these regularities be? His general answer developed from the concept of *anomie,* literally "normlessness." His theory assumed that for a morally ordered life and therefore an acceptance of one's role, men require a roughly regular, hence predictable, correlation between their norms for behavior and their objective possibilities to act. When there is great disjunction between the two, the result is a loss of meaningful limits—*anomie.* Individuals are disoriented, unable to predict and therefore uncertain about the future, and probably anxious. Rapid economic change effects such disjunction: in depression we cannot do objectively what we have learned we should do; in economic boom times, we can objectively do much more than our moral code, learned in a more Spartan past, allows. Thus the explanation is finally by analogy to our individual experience of deprivation and overindulgence.

It is noteworthy that one can accept Durkheim's laws without accepting his theory of social structure and *anomie.* Laws can force agreement, but we can, and do, differ on theory. Laws are organized by theory metaphorically, placed within a composition, a picture of the world that is larger in its significance and familiar because it is cognate with other experience. Theory relates laws to each other in a system that is meaningful to us as it resembles other and better understood systems.

Theory is, then, a constructed view of aspects of the world from which regularities can be deduced. It is logically consonant with, and implies, known laws. It explains them by including them in a larger regularity, and by ordering them in a pattern metaphorically familiar. And, equally important, it allows us to predict other, hitherto unknown laws.

From this the process of theory construction follows. We begin with what is known, with the invariant associations called laws. Without theoretical explanation they are merely "puzzles" for science. Brooding upon such laws, we speculate about relationships, borrowing metaphors as we are given to do. We construct a speculative theory, test it for internal order and fidelity to the known laws. Then we begin an intensive deductive examination of that theory. In this sense, theory predicts laws; we say "if this is so then such and so should also be."

The process of predicting new laws from theory rests upon a more precise specification of concepts. We make attributes, taken as constant in the original theory, problematic and variable. In considering the example of Durkheim's theory of *anomie,* one might ask: Given the disjunction between moral code and opportunity, given a state of *anomie,* what types of action could be expected to follow besides the extreme act of suicide? Robert K. Merton has pursued this line of thought with important results. But one could ask quite other questions: What happens if we look at Durkheim's original theory and vary societal attributes—say literacy? What happens if we vary the *rate* of rapid economic change? What happens if we vary both? The given theory may be expanded and changed in such manner.

Some have argued that though the aim of science is explanation and prediction, the former is merely a tool for the latter. This view is, in my opinion, diametrically opposite the truth. For me the aim is explanation, enlightenment concerning the order of our various experiences. The metaphorical nature of theory is its essence: it allows our various segregated experiences to approach integration, our map of the world, hence our philosophy, to gain a greater integrity. The purpose of prediction is to ground the explanation in the hard irreducible facts that make possible a more universal agreement on our human, hypothetical truth.

Norman Campbell, a physicist, puts the same position in different words:

the discovery of laws depends ultimately not on fixed rules but on the imagination of highly gifted individuals [and] this imaginative and personal element is much more prominent in the development of theories; the neglect of theories leads directly to the neglect of the imaginative and personal element in science. It leads to an utterly false contrast between "materialistic" science and the "humanistic" studies of literature, history and art.

At the heart of theory, which explains the laws of nature, lies the metaphor. Theories are forever untestable directly; only through the deduced laws and contrived hypotheses can we test them. Yet theory is the final aim of science: we want an empirically grounded theory of our experience in society and of it, so that we, in our philosophy, can relate that society to other important concerns.

[11]

MEASUREMENT AND
NUMERICAL LAWS

We are very lucky if we can formulate our laws in true mathematical language, for both generality and precision are extended by the process. Our descriptive laws necessarily become precise and, equally important, our relational laws increase in power. Furthermore, we are then able to use established mathematical forms to extend laws through combination with others; the relations among abstract numbers may suggest relationships among concrete measurable properties. These are of course empirically hypothetical, yet they have often been correct. The process of squaring a number was suggested by the nature of abstract number, not by observation of nature, yet it fits many theoretically important functions in the world.

The application of mathematics to empirical phenomena is not, however, simply a matter of our desire. Before we can do so we must establish true measurement of the object of inquiry and this requires that it conform to the abstract conditions, the rules, of true number. The nature of these rules is frequently misunderstood and therefore worth discussing.

The source of the misunderstanding is, as usual, confusion among the symbol, the concept, and the object. We use the same term for both symbol and concept; it will help if the first be called "numeral," leaving number for the concept representing an abstracted aspect of things. Thus we can refer to a given numerical collection in many ways; we use the symbol "5"; the Romans used "V," and the Greeks, ":·:". The concept, a collection of objects that can be counted off against the fingers of the usual human hand plus the thumb, is a number. (Further, it is an abstracted aspect of the concrete object, hand.)

At the essence of the concept number is the notion of "more than, less than." But of what? Essentially, of those aspects of things "which are changed by the combination of similar bodies." Mensurability then requires that when we combine two or more collections the sum change in orderly fashion. We can measure by matching volume, as in the Dahomean census; by matching weight, as in the use of a balance; by counting off particle against particle in two collections, as the fingers on two hands.

The rules for number are spelled out for that most abstract number, the series of numerals and their relations that we call mathematics. They are logical in their nature—a set of formal properties whose nature is assumed, whose relationships are implicit in their definition. Yet measurable properties of empirical objects must resemble the abstract property number if they are to be accurately represented by the same symbols, otherwise we violate the logical rule of identity in discourse.

To be measurable, an attribute must satisfy certain conditions. First, it must be empirically true that things equal to the same thing are equal to each other. If one person scores "5" on a scale, it must be equal to the "5" another scores, since both are represented by the same numeral, standing for a collection of five items. Second, when equals are added to equals the sums must be equal. Thus if two persons with five years completed in school each complete two more years the results must be equal. Finally, it must be possible, by expanding the magnitude of the collections symbolized by such numbers as 2, 5, 7, to find a collection that will describe any magnitude of the attribute numbered.

These aspects of things, the numerable aspects, are subject to empirical test. We judge equivalence through its effect upon some third object, and the effect we choose may vary widely— from the impact of a ray upon sensitized paper to the response of individuals with the same test scores to social situations. Thus we judge equivalence of volume by dimensions of containers, of weight by the angle of the scales' beam, of counting off particles by the agreement in sequence of the two matched collections—they stop at the same point in time.

The value of a numerical symbolic system, or numerals, is obvious in many ways. Having in general little resemblance to the concepts it stands for, it is not distracting; it has the identical advantages of language in these respects. Dealing only with the pure abstraction, number, it may be combined in shorthand, expanded, used to express the most complex relationships in precise but simplified form. It is a permanent, shared conceptual system expressed by symbols that remain stable in their meaning.

But it must be emphasized again that while number is an abstraction created and used by mathematicians, the measurement of the world is an empirical research effort. Before any measurement stands the hypothesis that the conditions of true number hold for the attributes to be described. Many of these attributes, abstracted from sense data through our frame of reference, are not measurable now and many may never be. Can we measure the velocity of action in dreams? Perhaps some day, perhaps not. It is obvious that measurement is a basic creative aspect of science, and research on measures, properly understood, of the greatest importance. With such instruments as the seismograph, a science may be founded.

But to repeat, measurement is not produced by simply willing it to be. It may be difficult indeed. In Campbell's words:

. . . measurement does depend upon experimental laws; . . . it does depend upon the facts of the external world; and . . . it is not wholly within our power to determine whether we will or will not measure a certain property.

What we can determine is the value of measurement, the evaluation of given kinds of description called measurement —and our own effort to discover aspects of things which resemble true number.

MEASUREMENT IN THE
SOCIAL SCIENCES

One of the greatest difficulties and opportunities in social science lies in the development of measurement. To put it briefly, our measures of many things of great theoretical importance do not satisfy the conditions of true number. We have at best crude approximations of measurement for such variables as *anomie* (critical to Durkheim's theory discussed earlier) sentiment, attitude, and the like. Yet we have theories that hypothesize invariant associations of these among themselves and with other aspects of behavior. We imagine the "felicific calculus" with units of happiness, but in practice we use crude questions for a crude concept.

The attributes of social life that do obey the rules of true number are frequently of marginal and questionable importance for our theories. We can deal with the number of animal bodies satisfying the descriptive laws for "human," but number of individuals alone is often not enough for reasonable statement, much less important theory. We can deal with clock time, but the equivalences do not relate to anything very meaningful. By what third criterion is the additional two years in school, endured by two persons who have already completed five years, an equivalence? Just in respect to hours logged? Wilensky has recently investigated the relationship between formal education and interest in "high culture"— science, philosophy and the arts—and he finds that additional years in school mean little until one deals with those who have graduated from a four-year college. Thus education is not a continuous variable in its effects, but rather a "step function."

What we can measure precisely is of marginal significance to our theory; what is critical cannot be measured according to the canons of true number. We are in danger of giving up the project of measurement entirely, of using spurious and misleading numerals, or acting like the drunk searching for his keys under the street lamp, not because he lost them there but because it is a more convenient place to search.

Yet the situation is not hopeless. In the first place, the search for true number in social attributes is a relatively recent one; its future success cannot be predicted on *a priori* grounds for, as we have noted, measurement rests upon experimental laws created through abstracting properties of the object.

For another thing, certain social attributes do indeed conform to the rules of true number. We might mention money in a market place. Measured by a third effect, say purchasing power, it has under many circumstances the attributes of equivalence, additivity, and completeness. It can be described by numerical laws and indeed has been with considerable success. One can of course point out that money is not always equal when tested against the market: the Negro's money is not as valuable as the white's in the housing market. But this merely requires that we specify the nature of the market more carefully.

In similar fashion, whenever we find social acts with identical consequences as measured by some third criterion, we can apply numerical laws. Thus the act of voting, however it is "motivated" in personality and "perceived" by the voter, results in one tally. And within a political community the aggregation of votes reflects an official finding of opinion, one that is an important attribute of that community. Of course it frequently determines who shall take office, what shall be done, but it is notable that the *margin* of victory is sometimes more important than the fact. Head counting, in other words, done in a framework of social action can be highly relevant to theoretical social science. The relevance may only hold for the third factor, but this is no proof of meaningless use of number: the measurement of weight tells us nothing about the object weighed. It may vary from orchids to artillery.

In the same way, the social events producing a given vote may vary, from financial interests on one actor's part to race prejudice on another's. Yet it is significant that we can predict from verbal evidence, weeks in advance, what the division of a vote will be. Further, we can predict with considerable efficiency if we know a few facts about the popula-

tion in the political community. The correlation between a
man's party preference and his vote is high; the correlation
between a man's preference and his parents' preference is also
very high. And the correlation with such social attributes as
social rank, life style, ethnic background, is high again.

But how does one measure these matters? Without going
into the techniques of attitude scale construction, question-
naire and interviewing (all dealt with very well in current
manuals of research procedures), let us say that we use approximate number. This is number derived from responses
to given acts of the social scientist, number that does not
satisfy the requirements of true number. Yet there is order;
one can say that with respect to some criterion, one act or
actor shows more than, or less than, another. This is ordinal,
or approximate, number.

Thus one could create a scale of "political predisposition,"
based upon the variables noted above. Lazarsfeld and his associates have done so, and have been able to account for a
considerable part of the variation in voting for national officials. Such scales usually will place one unit relative to a
second, yet they are very limited in their utility for more
complex numerical relationships: the interval between the
two units may not have any known relationship to that between the second and third units. Thus in the "social distance
scale," where people are asked "Would you work beside a
Negro," "would you live in a house beside that of a Negro,"
and "would you have a Negro relative," those who say yes
to the last question have the "least race prejudice," those who
say no to it but yes to the question of residence have "more,"
and those who say no to these plus the first question have
most. But whether the difference between the third and the
second equals that between the second and first we cannot
say: thus we cannot assume that equals added to equals will
produce equals. Yet we can say somehing about the three
classes we have distinguished by means of the scale.

There is another effort at measurement which we might
call "rhetorical number." This is the use of numerals to indicate classes or cases where nothing at all is known of the
order of the classes with respect to a criterion. It is most

charitably seen as a hypothesis, preceding the experimental test that will help to establish or falsify it as even a rough measure of what it is supposed to indicate. However, it is sometimes used in a purely nominal way, like the pagination in a book. To apply any sort of mathematical reasoning in such case is, of course, absurd.

It is apparent that the line between true number and approximate number is not always sharp and clear. It depends upon our purpose, our theoretical interest, whether a given attribute's measurement is adequate. If we are in a position to demand numerical laws of relationship, which our measurement of the object does not allow, then we have only approximate measures. And between approximate and rhetorical number the difference is one that can be established only by empirical experiment, studying the effects of variations, signified by numerals, upon a criterion class of objects or events.

Approximate numbers are very limited in their use for mathematically formulated laws of relationship. We can study covariation between two series, but our statement of that will be crude: we cannot specify with precision. But then, our social science theories do not usually require any very precise relations. As Campbell discusses laws in physical science, he notes that "The terms between which laws express relationships are themselves based on laws and represent collections of other terms related by laws." In truth, the laws of this latter sort are often barely noted in our research: the relation between a deviant's response to society and a societal response to deviation will become more clear as we understand the constituent laws of each of the units indicated. Yet more precise measurement might very well hasten that understanding.

MEASUREMENT AND TYPOLOGIES

Much of our applied mathematics was developed to describe and analyze laws that took a particular form: they were from physics and they were mechanical laws. The underlying metaphor is of a body acting upon a body with a given force. Yet it is clear that there are *other forms of law,* and that they are very important in the life sciences and the social sciences. As in geology we interpret the past through our knowledge of present processes and the structure now in existence (and explain what exists by theories of past events), so in physical anthropology we reconstruct the development of *homo sapiens* through laws based on the present but used in interpretation of fossils and other clues from the past. Might not the same model be applied to all human history, with existing society seen as a complex, stratified structure created by fission, eruption, erosion, in the past? The past would then be reconstructed through its remains in the present and analogous present events. Indeed, this is what we do, however informally and unconsciously we go about it.

Then there are the organic models used in the biological sciences. They have been extremely influential in some of the social sciences; their metaphor of the interaction between, on the one hand, an internally organized structure, which transforms energy in orderly ways and perpetuates itself and, on the other, its environment, is particularly appealing to those who study social groups. Yet the major laws involved in using this kind of theory are not mechanical in nature; they are typologies of structures, of environments, and of interactions between the two.

Whitehead speaks of classification as "a halfway house between the immediate concreteness of the individual thing and the complete abstraction of mathematical notions." He remarks that "unless you can progress from classification to mathematics, your reasoning will not take you far." But the use of types does not preclude the use of mathematics. The typology is best used as an element of *theory,* and from that theory one should be able to deduce laws, statements of invariant relations that may be formulated in mathematical terms and tested empirically. And to begin with, a typology should specify descriptive laws that have a precise mathematical formulation: between the necessary attributes of the type there should be a correlation described by a coefficient of 1.0.

In short, types represent in themselves invariant association.

Max Weber was one of the first sociologists to introduce the profession to hard thought on the subject. Using historical data, he constructed "ideal types," by which he meant generic descriptions of social forms stated in very extreme terms so as to identify their attributes and separate them from other forms. In his usage, no particular case would exactly fit an ideal type, yet the case would be illuminated by the characteristics of the type it was identified with. Perhaps his best known ideal type is the bureaucracy.

The ideal typical bureaucracy is a kind of formal social structure. The "office" within the organization is quite separate from any person occupying it; the person is responsible to others in a chain of command, and vice versa; his key acts are recorded, and his accountability guaranteed by the process of review by others; authority within the organization is strictly by formal rules and position; and so on. Thus Weber illuminated the enormous differences between a tribe or a feudality on one hand, and the modern army, state, or corporation on the other.

Contemporary students of organization, however indebted to Weber for many of the major elements in their thought, have gone far beyond his "ideal typology." They have used his ideal type as the basis for descriptive laws, and from these have created the "constructed type." This is the empirically testable set of descriptive laws that identifies a bureaucracy. Such laws are usually not simple Aristotelian dichotomies—they are variables. That is, we measure the degree and nature of accountability, separation of the office from the person in it, and the like. (However crude the measure, it indicates the variable nature of the attribute.) From such measurement we can then go on to ask questions about the internal relationships of the components of the bureaucracy: What is the relationship between accountability and the separation of roles? (Generally, positive.) We then proceed to ask what difference it makes in the effect of the bureaucracy when given items vary: What is the relation between accountability and efficiency? (As Blau and others indicate, very complex and dependent on the formal task of the bureaucracy.)

Thus number can enter into our constructed types in very important ways. It can help us to construct those empirical laws by which we identify types and discriminate among them. And as our variables become more nearly measurable, as they resemble true number, we are able to develop more precise and subtle variations within types. Numerical laws can also be used to relate the type to third variables and in the process improve its mensurability. At a macroscopic scale, we might be interested in comparing degrees of bureaucratic organization in various enterprises with the kind and amount of innovation in each. (Thus the railroads might be compared with the communications industry in the United States.)

A common use of number with typology occurs in the sample survey. With a descriptive law for given types of object or event, one samples a relevant universe (say the adult population of the United States.) He can then compare social types (say, Negroes and whites) with respect to other attributes that interest him. He may then develop relational laws between different types of events, stating them in statistical form, say the correlation between race and propensity to vote.

It is worth noting that the invariant association described by statistical laws is an invariance of proportions, not of wholes. Thus the correlation between education and propensity to vote does not mean that no uneducated persons vote, and all college graduates do. Yet it yields important information, for the relation between the two attributes is very consistent. Much of the variation in propensity to vote is associated with race, as more Negroes than whites are apt to vote Democratic; this should not be confused by saying "Negroes are more democratic than whites," for those who are Republican may be just as much so as anybody. When comparing proportions of a given type, we are doing just that: we are saying nothing about the remainder in that category.

To do so we would have to prove that the proportion reflects a variable in each individual—that the proportion of
women giving birth to children reflects the degree of preg-
nancy in the population of women. (This may strike the
reader as obvious, but it is remarkable how often such hidden
assumptions creep into the interpretation of sample survey
results.)

The aim of the enterprise is, of course, to test theory by
discovering that its laws are correct. Precise prediction is
the test. But it is important to remember that precise prediction is a tricky concept, having several meanings. One may
say that there are no laws in social science, for prediction is
always statistical, with the kinds of "error" noted above. This
position assumes that precision demands that all the variance of the event we are interested in be accounted for by
the laws we use to predict it. If, however, we are not using
all the laws sufficient for such prediction, it is still possible
that the law we *are* using is necessary for prediction. In short,
we may not be able to predict all voting by using education,
but anyone who wishes to predict voting will have to take
education into account.

One way of expanding the amount of variance accounted
for, and thus improving our prediction, is by asking the old
question: Under what circumstances does education *not* relate
to voting in the predicted fashion? We then add qualifications,
specified conditions. But these may be turned into variables,
limiting the extent of the law as originally formulated, but
expanding the general theory through additional laws.

Our measures are crude and our theoretical constructions
have far outrun them. Many aspects of bureaucracy are measured with great difficulty and it is impossible to gain universal agreement on their usefulness. With this difficulty in
measuring the variables that as a cluster in a given order
stand for the constructed type "bureaucracy," it is impossible
to state all relevant aspects of bureaucracy in comparable numerical form. We simply have a set of approximate measures
and there is a temptation to use those that prove the case.

Under the circumstances it is very difficult to combine,

compare, to vary symbolically but precisely the theory. Some have decided that, with the very nature of social structure so difficult to measure in terms that satisfy the rules of number, we shall have to have a new set of mathematical laws—a set more congruent with the nature of the typologies we use. We have, on one hand, enormous regularities in social life but, on the other, a looseness vexing to the scientist (qua scientist, not necessarily as citizen). Thus far, the greatest progress in creating numerical laws has been through the development of statistics, which seem in certain ways congruent with the behavior of social aggregates. But those who aspire to greater precision and believe the difficulty is in our mathematics argue that we must have a *new* mathematics for social science.

Nobody can know: it is an empirical question. Mathematics proposes, the nature of social structure disposes.

[12]

MODELS, THEORIES,
AND GUIDING METAPHORS

After the end of World War II there arose among the primitive societies of the south Pacific a phenomenon called "cargo cults." These were quasi-religious efforts to recapture the wealth and foreign delicacies that had been theirs as a result of occupation by armies of the "advanced" societies. The cargo cults constructed, albeit with primitive materials and designs, facsimiles of the docks and landing strips where the laden ships and planes had arrived. It was held as a matter of faith that, once their homes were created, the cargo bearers would appear.

A similar phenomenon occurs in social science when practicing sympathetic magic we commune in the Cargo Cults of Methodology. Facsimiles of methods developed in more mature sciences are hastily thrown up, using such materials as come to hand. In the last chapter we noted one such cult—the cult of quantification, issuing in the creation of Rhetorical Number. Here the communicants, needing to quantify and unable to do so, create facsimiles of number through the assignment of numerals; imagining Bentham's "felicific calculus," they may measure hedonic temperature by asking if one is "Very Happy, Happy, So-So, Unhappy, or Very Unhappy." To the results are then attached numerals and we are off on a multiple regression analysis.

Similar cargo cults have appeared with respect to the conceptual realm and thus the high regard in which social scientists hold axiomatic theory, mathematical theory, models, and mathematical models. Since there is little uniformity in the way these terms are used, perhaps it will be useful to adopt a terminology. We will then be in position to see what has been accomplished in these directions by social scientists and what might be done under what circumstances.

By axiomatic theory we mean a completely circular axiomatic system. Given the definitions of terms and operations, all propositions are logically implied and one can start at any point and specify relations among the other terms. Euclidean geometry is such a system: the implications of its axioms are not by any means self-evident, yet they can be teased out through logical calculation; in this sense, all of an axiomatic theory is a unity.

Such a theory need not have any particular reference to empirical reality. It is a matter of strict conceptual order and closure. But when it is meant to be empirically testable it is then termed an "interpreted" theory; here its identification, measurement, and statements of law refer to the world of sense data. It is not necessary (and indeed, not possible) that they all do so, but certain critical propositions point to aspects of empirical reality and thus allow the possibility that we can falsify the theory. Euclid's theory serves admirably as illustration, for it is falsifiable when used to measure physical reality, yet rarely falsified.

There are no axiomatic, satisfactorily interpreted, theories in the social sciences. Perhaps the closest is a low-level theory in demography—one that takes the terms birth, death, immigration, and emigration, and from them generates propositions about the state and rate of growth or decline in a given human population. But while the theory is circular, it does not traverse a large enough circle to be particularly interesting, and it finally rests not upon social theory, but upon some brute facts of biology. Populations grow by reproduction or immigration, decline by mortality and emigration.

Earlier social scientists searched for a philosopher's stone in the shape of a single axiomatic theory of human social behavior, parallel to Newtonian theory in physics. With the exception of Talcott Parsons, who will be discussed later, this approach has been abandoned. Today we struggle for what Merton calls "middle range theory," a tightly integrated argument referring to some tightly integrated aspect of social life, some island of orderly association, some cluster of invariants.

The problem in constructing social theory is, on the surface, the problem of interpretation, of developing adequate empirical referents. But it is often equally obvious that the nature of the theory itself, its weak and blurred terms (e.g., "happiness"), transferred from the folk language, prevents precise empirical description. Zetterberg's efforts to axiomatize Durkheim would be much more convincing if we had any idea of what is meant, in precise terms, by such concepts as "solidarity," "interaction," and the like. Until these are adequately specified, interpretation will be as varied as individual hunches, while measurement will be, to put it mildly, highly pluralistic. A strait focus upon one segment of behavior may produce results (as with learning theory in the psychological sciences), but it will require cooperation between social scientists and social reality (and the cooperation of the latter is by no means guaranteed).

Until recently social scientists were content to work toward axiomatic theory. In recent years, nevertheless, there has been increasing interest in the development of something called the "mathematical model." The term model is used, however, in various senses. In the policy sciences it is sometimes used to refer to ideal conditions—model behavior by model people. It is sometimes just a way of referring to fairly abstract theory. And it sometimes refers to the process of quantifying laws.

It seems most sensible to use the term "model" to refer to a developed theory that is isomorphic to an undeveloped one. A mathematical model would then be a developed theory for which quantitative values can be stated, values for the description of both variables and relations among them. In this sense, mathematical models are of little value for social science except in those areas where variables conform to the demands of true number; otherwise isomorphism is not determinable. As we have noted in the previous chapter, such areas are rare.

To be sure, the creation of mathematical models is a modish enterprise in some disciplines. And within the strictures noted, it may be fruitful. *If* one has true measurement of variables, and *if* one can conduct partial analysis in which there are not too many unknowns interfering with the behavior he analyzes, it is possible to proceed. Linear programming, a way of combining many independent variables to predict outcomes, has had some success in economic analysis. But when the conditions do not hold the exercise can easily become an example of art for art's sake. I once saw a ten-page linear program meant to determine the effect of transportation investment on the economic development of an African nation. An anthropologist raised the question of the impact of social structure—specifically, what of people who live in a nonmonetary economy, what of the existence in fact of a *dual* economy, where tribe and city exist in uneasy symbiosis? The model builder pointed to a Greek symbol down in the lower right-hand corner of the last page and stated that this variable represented "social structure." Unfortunately, the latter was critical for his problem, and it presented entirely too many unknowns for him to solve by using the sparse quantifiable "knowns."

Although models, if rigorously defined, have presently a very limited use in social science, the term "model" is ubiquitous. One could dismiss this popularity as merely a fad, a new cargo cult, if there did not seem to be a common meaning underlying all the usages noted. This use of "model" would seem to indicate a configurative concept that can be used in widely varying circumstances. It is a formal abstraction, like any complex concept, and its utility varies with the empirical nature of its referent.

In common usage, then, we are not talking about formal models most of the time. We are really talking about something that precedes formalization, precedes axiomatic and formal theory. We are in fact using a controlling conceptual scheme, one that is purely formal and without content, one that may *lead* to the construction of empirical theory. Let us be clear: model, as we use it in social science, simply refers to a *guiding metaphor*.

Guiding metaphors are created by analogizing. Forms useful in other contexts are applied to the problem at hand; they are forms that lead us to abstract certain aspects in terms of their interrelations in the observed event. Thus Whitehead uses the term "organism" to refer, indifferently, to the interrelation of parts among animate and inanimate objects, man and social events. In social science we use the term "stratification" to refer to the persistent hierarchical division of societies by occupation, education, and the like—in short, by rights and duties assigned; the term is an adaptation of a geological concept referring to the layers of matter on the earth. But it is important to see that the formal concept of stratification is not limited in its reference to earth or social classes: indeed, it has no specific content.

A guiding metaphor can generate a wide range of concrete theories, depending upon the area of application. Geological stratification is one thing, social stratification among humans or chickens another, while the stratification of language in a garbled text, such as the Bible, is another matter again. We might say that the essence of the guiding metaphor is an abstract concept, its concrete use a "private" conception of the discipline involved and (to begin with) a private conception of the individual social scientist.

Concrete theories usually result from known (or assumed) laws ordered by guiding metaphors. The laws may be as simple as the descriptive laws for a kangaroo, the metaphor may consist in human consciousness and purpose, and the resulting theory, anthropomorphism, may be a simple transfer of human characteristics to the nonhuman. The laws may be as complex as theories of magic and the supernatural. In any event, they are tested against what is known or assumed and, if they account for the known facts, accepted.

Scientific theory requires, as we have seen, rather more. Here the criteria for correspondence between events and theory are more rigorous, and the theory should not only account for all known facts, it should predict new regularities. The roots are, however, similar. Out of the guiding metaphor combined with existing knowledge emerges folk theory, and out of that, scientific theory. The latter may depart far from the folk notions: it may reach the stage where its only obvious guiding metaphor is the pure mathematical structure, as seems largely true of the new physics.

No matter what the guiding metaphor, its translation into a theory or even a model determines its usefulness. All that is not translated is left out, a fuzzy residual of connotation—at most a source of future insights. Thus when we transfer a true model to a new subject matter, we must be certain to include all the elements necessary for the explanatory and predictive power the original had, or take the risk of founding another cargo cult. To interpret a mathematical structure that requires continuous variables in a social situation where they do not exist or cannot be measured is to court such danger.

SOME GUIDING METAPHORS IN
SOCIAL SCIENCE

Since the process of metaphorical thought is a formal one, it is clear that the range of possible guiding metaphors is practically infinite. However, in trying to answer the questions: what moves men? what maintains society? a few metaphors have been of outstanding importance. These include the meteorological, the game, the machine, and the organism.

The meteorological metaphor has been important in social psychology, especially in analyses of public opinion and popular culture. In translation, it leads us to see individuals as moved by drives organized into social attitudes, or "tendencies to act." These meet within the individual in what have been called "vectors of mind," and result in social action. They are conceived as responding to laws similar to the parallelogram of forces or multiple factor determination.

In this view the collective is an aggregate of biological individuals with shared attitudes, or culture. They pass these attitudes on to each other and to the next generation through
contact. The "weather" may change a great deal, opinions
may shift radically in response to external events, in much
the same way that a cold front changes the temperature of a
city; the shift in opinions about Nazi Germany after the
declaration of war in 1941 was such a dramatic shift. Potential
attitudes were activated, others suppressed. But while the
weather changes, the "climate of opinion" remains relatively
constant.

Change in attitudes does not progress uniformly throughout the population, nor does the whole complex of attitudes
change in an orderly and consistent fashion. Thus we have
conflict between groups differing in attitude, and conflict
within the individual. Myrdal used some such metaphor
when he spoke of the position of Negroes in the United
States as "An American Dilemma," for racist attitudes and
egalitarian attitudes were in violent conflict. The parallelogram of forces has changed since he wrote, but the "vectors"
remain the same: only the values of the variables have shifted.

The metaphor of the game is associated with the work of
George Herbert Mead, a philosopher turned social psychologist. Unlike the meteorological style of social psychology, he
emphasizes the rules that order relationships among the
players into conceptual and empirical wholes. In this view,
the individual player is maximizing his values within given
rules, in cooperation with members of his team and competi-
tion with the "others"—who may be inanimate, nature. The
collective is, then, a social circle or team or set of teams,
playing within rules established by the "generalized other,"
which is, in the individual, conscience reinforced by expectations of how others will judge him. Thus the statement: you
can predict more of a ball player's actions through a knowledge of the rules and strategy of baseball than through all
theories of personality combined.

But within the given rules and strategies there are still enormous variations in action and outcome. The plays have vary-

ing effects and their outcomes produce a change in possible futures, as do completed games. Skills and basic potentials vary in realization, grow and decline. But the nature of the game remains relatively constant so that, over short time periods, it can generally be considered fixed. The metaphor of the game has been used extensively in the study of international relations, labor-management relations, and other inter-organizational problems. It has been extended through the construction of games that simulate given aspects of a problem area: so there are "management games," "legislative games," and "international relations games."

But the rules and strategies of the serious games of social life do change, often gradually but sometimes abruptly. Change may produce anarchy, with discrepant rules controlling different players. (When baseball was first introduced to the Philippines one batter, disliking the umpire's call, turned around and brained him with his bat.) Changes in strategy also produce disorder for the predictor, for a kind of communication has been broken down. Hybrid games result in the real world, until the time when formalization is resumed. The applicability of the metaphor is limited by these considerations.

In the metaphor of the machine, the individual is seen as a fixed, moving part. He is fixed by his social position, he moves by the specification of his role, and he is controlled by his interaction with other fixed moving parts. In this metaphor the order of the factory has been transferred to its human machine-tenders. The collective is, then, a social machine. It is constrained by its internal order and directed toward the environment, something like a giant lawmower fueled by the grass it cuts. It is a mechanical energy transformation system.

Now machines typically move through cycles, so a machine may be seen at any phase of its cycle. Its periodicity has to be known if the full cycle is to be discovered and the meaning of a given phase understood: that meaning will be a function of the full cycle. But the structure of the machine changes very slowly and thus we have a structure whose function is knowable. The reason for individual behavior is given in its function within the social machine.

This metaphor is popular in many areas of social inquiry. Whether one is concerned with the function of the extended family in the Trobriand Islands or the staff-line conflict in modern bureaucracies, it tends to lurk beneath the discourse. Industrial sociology, military science, business administration, all focus upon the workings and well-being of social machines.

Change in the social machinery produces stripped gears and breakdowns. Hence the metaphor leads one to buy new parts (change personnel), to fit old ones better (in-service training) or invent entirely new rigs (the new department, the created job). Or one may refuse to tinker with details and try to design entirely new machinery. In the area of political science called public administration, emphasis is upon the craft of repair and adjustment, but one often senses a deep yearning for entirely new models—utopias. Constitution-drafting is, in this viewpoint, analogous to the making of blueprints. Implementing constitutions is, of course, another matter; those who are committed to the social machine metaphor sometimes seem to yearn for a more standard and predictable human part, in a more nicely constraining system; it would greatly improve the validity of their social science. And indeed, nature does copy art, as Hitler demonstrated.

Perhaps the oldest metaphor for society is that of the organism. Here we look at a society as a functionally integrated whole, living in the sense that it grows, declines, and is reproduced through time, learns and forgets. The individual is a cell, and like a cell lives and dies within a larger, persisting structure, the organ. The cell's nature is determined by the organ within which it exists and it is controlled by that nature interacting with other cells within the overall plan of the organ.

The collective is, in turn, a set of interdependent organs, or social groups. These are specialized for their functions and each is necessary for the whole: that necessity is then a basis for both empirical theory and normative prescription. The story of the hand that cut the throat to spite the stomach occurs many times in many places. And specific social organisms, or societies, do commit suicide, just as they grow quantitatively and change qualitatively. They prosper, sicken and die, like organs and individuals.

The species is relatively constant though, and knowledge of it can be transferred to other members. Its nature specifies the limits for the "body social." But there is evolution, variation, and change in the very nature of the beast. Through what Donald Campbell calls "blind variation and selective retention" of what is advantageous, individuals, groups, and whole societies evolve. While physical mutation is relatively unimportant, there is analogous mutation in ideas, brought about by the combination and permutation in the individual mind of cultural strains and symbolic transformations.

Durkheim is one of the most important social scientists to exploit the organic metaphor. He points to the simplest societies as analogous to very simple organisms. Consisting of many similar units (bands, tribes, villages), each quite self-sufficient, half the society may be destroyed and the remainder, like a tapeworm, will reconstitute the old size and shape again. But with the merging of many small societies in a larger order, the very structure of social life changes; the subunits become specialized, dependent upon others for most of life's necessities, and we have moved from a "mechanical" to an "organic" species. The metaphor has changed and the fact of interdependence, together with the corollary, vulnerability of the whole, becomes a central concern.

Using this metaphor, change can be said to produce hybrid organisms and new species. It also produces "survivals" of an earlier form; as the human body has been called a museum of biological antiquities, so any society is a museum of cultural antiquities. (We wear buttons on our coat sleeves because a British admiral did not want his men to use their coat sleeves for handkerchiefs.) Growth and change in the society is by no means allomorphic; there is no necessary fit in the change of scale occurring in the family structure, the economic structure, and the polity. Thus it is possible to produce monsters and freaks, giants and dwarfs. And one may use the pathological metaphor, if he knows what true health would be for the given species.

And we could discuss other metaphors. There is the dramatic metaphor that sees the play as the thing, the content of roles in the developing plot and concern for the audience. There is the hydraulic metaphor, much favored by historians, which sees waves and tides move through an underlying "human nature." There are the vague and powerful metaphors of philosophers, estheticians, moralists—essences, inner meanings, ultimates, ghosts, and archetypes. But the ones discussed above are samples that will do and are, I think, presently most influential.

The question arises: How do you choose a guiding metaphor? One answer is that, usually, you don't. You are apt to take them for granted and fail even to recognize them as metaphors. Then you will adopt the metaphors given by the conventions of thought in your discipline or by common sense. Thus the phrases, "the political game," "the social body," "the climate of opinion," "the military machine." These are commonplace shifts of meaning from folk toward technical language.

But guiding metaphors are powerful limits and directives for the resulting theories. They highlight that which conforms, and they suppress "irrelevant" aspects; they can lead to a kind of theoretical "tunnel vision." Thus we can ask of the four discussed above: How do they handle change? In the metaphor of the social machine, change is a matter of either attrition and breakdown, or conscious human tinkering with design and detail; in the organic metaphor it is much less consciously produced and systematically effected. We can also ask: What are the limits of applicability? The game metaphor is limited to situations where there are rules and strategies which allow prediction and communication among the players, but much of history consists of confrontation between groups and individuals playing quite different games, mutually unintelligible, or games that hardly mesh. Christian missionaries were welcomed in the Scandinavian north with open arms, for they could be sold immediately for slaves. And the organic metaphor, useful as it is, still refers to a peculiar organism when applied to society—one in which the cells can wander from organ to organ, or even from organism to organism, without either cell or organism suffering.

What are the criteria for choosing metaphors? Simply relevance to the problem. There is empirical control—its relevance to observations—and logical control—its relevance to other concepts. For the metaphor is a halfway house, like the type, and the final aim is to create a systematic theory congruent with empirical realities. And that theory may, finally, be expressible only through mathematics, its metaphor a structure of concepts represented by mathematical notation.

[13]

EXPLANATION
AND THE DELIMITATION
OF A SCIENTIFIC FIELD

An eminent criminologist once explained the origin of the "eclectic theory" of juvenile delinquency causation. In his view, it grew out of the institution of crime commissions, which included welfare workers, sociologists, economists, psychologists, and so on. Each kind of practitioner argued vigorously for the importance of "his" variables in producing delinquency. The result was a gentleman's agreement to divide up the pie-chart of causation, with a certain per cent of delinquency allocated to broken families, a certain per cent to poverty, a certain per cent to "deep-seated personality problems." The resulting jurisdictions were not irrelevant: they were reflected in budgetary allocations for attacking the social problem of crime committed by youth.

Here we have a parody of the delineation of scientific fields, yet it is not altogether farfetched. If one looks at the curriculum of the social sciences in a major university, he finds departments of economics (studying social production and distribution of values), of political science (studying maintenance of social order), of sociology (studying organization of groups, which in turn produce and distribute values, maintain social order) of anthropology (studying similar groups, usually distinguished only by their lack of alphabet and breeches), and so on. In short, these are variations of disciplines that make little sense except as convention; like the crime commissions, the social sciences reflect in their organization the growth of competing groups, rather than the growth of intellectual order.

How then do we define a scientific field? From this question the next follows: What is the business of a social science? The question is not purely "academic," for it touches the integrity of the disciplines as well as the work norms: Who is responsible for what? There are two general approaches; one begins with the empirically known, the other with the theoretical frame of reference we bring to it.

ORDERLY PHENOMENA

One may define the subject matter of a science through indicating the orderly phenomena it is concerned with. These are regularities in human experience that are apprehended through existing concepts and the problem is, given the existence of these regularities, what causes them and what follows from them. Given the rate of juvenile delinquency in the community, explain it, and in the explanation should lie the key to changing it. This approach frequently begins with "social problems."

But where do the definitional laws come from? In general, they come out of the accumulated lore, observation, and categories of the larger society: thus we study "marriage and the family," "race relations," "legislative behavior," or "the theory of the firm." Such concepts may not, however, carry us very far; as Lemert's work demonstrates, they are apt to be unanalyzed abstractions. Still they are starting points for inquiry (see chapter 10).

Once the regularities have been discovered and described precisely, the next step is explanation. Explanation may come from any concepts at hand, any notions possibly applicable. The aim is to "explain all cases," and it is usually interpreted as predicting all cases—that is, finding a set of laws that, taken together, describe all juvenile delinquents. The result may very well be a mess of mixed metaphors, with the individual's psyche (conscious and unconscious), his social participation, his economic and ethnic status, all thrown together in a linear program aimed at "accounting for" delinquency.

About any given class of events one may ask a number of questions that lead to the search for laws. For example, what do you want to explain about a social group such as a labor union? One approach is to account for its *origins*. There was an aggregate of people and it became organized in a certain predictable way. We can begin with the difference between original invention of the "union complex" and learning from others about the nature of unions. Then we can go on to the creation of order through shared responses to a situation, the emergence of leadership, the resulting creation of a role system. Then we can investigate the requisites for leadership, personality of the leader, responses of followers. In one union, a critical factor in its original success may have been the character and personality of a major employer, so one must investigate these variables, as well as the job market, consumption standards among the putative members, and so on *ad infinitum*.

But then we can also ask: How does this given order among an aggregate of individuals *maintain* itself? What is there about the structure that repeats itself over time; what are the processes and trends of change? What of formal constraints and informal, of collusion between management and the union hierarchy? What of personal relations among the leadership, friendships and feuds? What are the symbolic satisfactions of the members, as against their financial gains or losses? What importance does the union have as a system of lawful order counterbalancing management's drive to maximize profits?

As a third strategy, we can ask: What are the *effects* of this organized group upon nonorganizational variables? Does membership in the union result in changes in the individual's personality, does it increase self-respect and diminish *anomie*? And, going further, what are the consequences of this particular kind of group for other kinds, ignoring individuals as such? What does the presence of a strong set of local unions do for the political structures of a given community?

When we start with the existence of orderly phenomena (which lie all about us) we can go in an infinite number of directions. There is no guide as to which is preferable save trial and error or personal taste. The result of this approach is usually an empirical science closely tied to everyday concerns, one that studies the metropolitan area with concepts not far different from those used by a real estate agent, or juvenile delinquency in the vocabulary of the probation officer.

EXPLANATORY THEORY

When a scientific field is *theoretically* delimited, the emphasis is upon its explanatory laws. These in turn yield the descriptive laws, for they describe the aspects of a class of things the laws are meant to explain. In the welter of possible experience represented by the social phenomenon called "labor union," an organizational sociologist would be interested only in those social actions constrained and directed by the laws of organization. For these, having their own order in a theory of organization, are the subject matter of his discipline. The results of internal control systems in the representation of ethnic minorities in the union's leadership, and the consequences of such representation for the control system, might be such an interest. The psychological problems of a Negro union leader, torn between loyalty to an ethnic group and loyalty to the union hierarchy, would not be. (He would be seen as simply an actor whose multiple roles might, on occasion, produce conflict between fields of force, making for erratic leadership.)

In this kind of approach, explanation is acceptable *only* in terms of the theoretically delimited discipline. This limit does not mean that other classes of events are not relevant to the concrete events, the sociologist studies; they are just not relevant to his conceptual problems. A student of community social organization does not study geography and meteorology (although a flood can certainly affect a community's social structure), for the prediction of floods and their physical courses are highly complex matters in their own right, not explicable by social theory. What he will be able to study is the reaction of the community to flood or the danger of flood, for this grows from analysis of social structure and affects it in turn. The "flood" will be subsumed under concepts internal to his theory. It is a class of disaster, while disaster may be conceived of as the incidence of threats so multitudinous and/or sudden as to exceed, at least temporarily, the community's capabilities for organized response.

The aim is to deal with only one level of theory at a time, resulting in one set of abstracted aspects of the subject of study. Further, one chooses the subject in terms of its relevance to these theoretically delimited aspects and no other. One student of organizational theory, James Moorhead, was chiefly interested in the relations among several organizational systems overlapping within the same aggregate of individuals. He chose the interaction of union and management in work groups in the building construction industry. He discovered that protection of the workers' interest could be predicted by a simple datum: when the role of union steward and foreman were separate the workers' interests were maximized, when collapsed into one role, minimized. (The workers' main concern was freedom to do a craftsmanlike job; when the roles of steward and foreman were merged the value of a craftsmanlike job was slighted in the interest of quantity.) This relationship was, despite the simplicity of measures, highly predictive. Yet the sociologist's interest was not in the craft interests of workers, nor in the quality of construction; it was in the effects of two potentially separate fields of control on the same concrete group. He was working with "facts that are symbols, and laws that are their explanation."

The delimitation of a field of inquiry by explanatory theory raises a number of important questions. In the first case, what must you assume as constant (or at least controllable) from other levels of conceptualized reality? This is the problem of partial analysis again. Do you have to account for individual and collective learning in detail? Personality structure? In short, how do you relate the levels of explanation?

A number of strategies are used (some are discussed earlier; see chapter 10). One is to assume, for your purposes, "standard men." While you know this is not exactly true, you minimize variation by matching the general characteristics of people in different groups. The rationale is that despite considerable individual variation, if the laws you discover are powerful the argument for them is increased by the knowledge that other variables are confounding the results. If I can say, regardless of the history and ideology of their leaderships, unions whose polity is organized in certain forms will consistently have more (or less) membership participation than those organized otherwise, I have an argument.

Closely kin to this strategy is that of randomizing samples. This is another way to get at "standard men," but here one is, in effect, trying to describe standard populations. Allowing each sample the same probability of including the intelligent, the stupid, the freak and conformist, one hopes that such variations are canceled out in the final result. This can often be checked by measuring the similarity of samples and variations within them. (Such a check will, however, be only as adequate as the measures.)

Finally we should always remember the likelihood that our system of laws is not adequate at the single level and should be expanded. The "exogenous variable," completely outside the system of explanation, may be redefined in terms of its relevance for the "endogenous variables" of our theory. From flood to disaster to a class of events having specified consequences for a community is such a translation. In similar fashion we translate from "railroads and airplanes," to "transportation," to the conditions for interaction and integration among human populations. This last is internal to sociological theory, the first are folk concepts. They may be studied by transportation engineers interested in programming empty freight cars, by physicists interested in energy transformation, or by environmental scientists interested in air pollution. No given item, *none*, has a single fixed meaning. Its significance is a result of the interpretive framework used. There is no such thing as a "social datum" or a "psychological datum"; there are simply sociological and psychological frames of reference that give meaning to data.

Finally, theoretical delimitation of a field raises the problem: How much predictive power *should* you expect, given a theory admittedly partial? The answer is that you do not know *a priori*. Your work norms remain open-ended. Most scientists would hope for very accurate prediction for the classes of events studied by the laws as formulated: they would hope that, with an adequate *set* of laws they could account for all variance.

SOME ARGUMENTS FOR EACH APPROACH

There are respectable arguments for each of these approaches. Some prefer to go about looking for interesting regularities in social life, and then to seek explanations. Others prefer development of interesting ideas about society and a consequent search for documentation, proof, and the crucial experimental conditions. It is in part a matter of style; given our need for both a knowledge of regularities and explanations for them, the statesmanlike position would be support of a random strategy, or every man to his own taste. However, the arguments for each approach are worth stating.

Those who believe the task is defined by orderly regularities point out that most science begins with careful observation using a common-sense vocabulary. Astronomy began with the observed regularities of the heavenly bodies at a time when they were still conceived as deities; economics began with the problems of financing the state. Thus we must be willing to allow any class of invariants as a possible basis for a set of laws and theories. "Social problems" like the incidence of juvenile delinquency are as good points of departure as any.

Then, the argument follows, out of a sufficient collection of laws, theories can eventually be developed as explanation. Obviously this position goes back at least as far as Bacon; it counsels careful and precise observation of a sufficient number of instances. Proponents of the position may adduce the work of Tycho Brahe, the early astronomer who was a great measurer and through measurement made accessible a world of data used to test the theories of a Copernicus, Galileo, or Newton. But let us remember that Brahe happened on a fruitful puzzle: Why are there such orderly patterns among the heavenly bodies? Yet the puzzle was not really solved by Brahe; it was documented by him. And the range of possible documentation is enormous—including much that is scientifically sterile. (One might classify plants by the color of their blossoms, people by the color of their hair.)

The argument for a theoretically delimited approach rests, pragmatically, on the necessity for a division of labor among social scientists. Few can be really competent in more than one approach and it does not help matters to have sociologists bolstering their arguments with obsolete psychology or vice versa. By rigorous limitation of intellectual responsibility we can escape the dreadful predicament of having to know *every-thing* about the subject at hand.

There is also a real value in an intense commitment to a fruitful insight. The work of Marx and Freud did not profit from encyclopedic knowledge of human behavior but from their *limitation* of vision. Compared with these the great eclectics such as Gaetano Mosca, however agreeable their work to common sense, failed to add to our knowledge in comparable fashion. There is much to be said for intellectual celibacy, disciplinary fixation: the determination to perfect a theory orderly in its structure and ruthless in its implications.

Until we have developed strength, analytical and empirical, in the various social sciences, relations among their laws remain highly problematic. We could say that, given confusion in the economics of the firm, confusion in the sociology of administration, and confusion in our theories of personality, adding them together simply results in confusion raised to a higher power. This is the great and, I believe, insuperable difficulty faced by such theorists as Talcott Parsons. His effort to integrate "social, cultural, and personality systems" suffers from our very rudimentary achievements in understanding each. Before we can have interdisciplinary approaches we must have discipline. We can imagine "cross-sectional laws," invariants relating the psychological, cultural, and sociological invariants; first we must develop the latter.

It is useful to consider two quite separate dimensions in any given science. The first we might call the analytic–synthetic. By the analytic we mean pure theory—How do you explain? What units are analyzed? What is the form of your laws? By the synthetic we mean the nature of the scientific frame as it is applied to the many-dimensional world. It is the answer to the question: What class of events are you interested in?

At the same time, sciences vary by their degree of development, from folk thought to internally significant bodies of empirically grounded theory. The latter can say a great deal more about the world because they are made up of *statements of relationships,* culminating in abstractive hierarchies whose concepts have wide generality and specific empirical implications. Thus the development of the analytic, the conceptual realm, may be an indication of a movement toward "internally significant" bodies of theory. But it may merely be an effort to say at once all the simple descriptive laws, at best leaving statements of relations among them metaphorical and so avoiding the difficulty of interpretation. In this case it is simple convention—a classification, a literary conceit, a substitute for science.

In the study of human behavior there seem to be at present two major analytical frameworks. There have been many proffered in the past—the biological–evolutionary, the geographical, the moral–theological—but of these the survivors are, today, social science and psychological science. The first takes the laws of social aggregates as the basis for explanation, with the fate of individual and concrete group a dependent variable. Psychology, on the other hand, takes the nature of the individual as a theoretically closed system for its basic explanation, with social behavior as the dependent variable.

But the conventionally defined disciplines of social science may not have a fixed relation to these analytically defined approaches. They may use either or both of them, for they may be defined in terms of their *synthetic* reference, got directly out of common-sense discourse. Thus the field of "Government," which became "Politics," which became "Political Science," today includes scientists and research reports of both points of view. It ranges from psychological studies of "political socialization" to sociological studies of "organizational behavior."

Nor is this mixture of approaches to be deplored. The true growth of the social sciences centers around developing analytical theory that can be interpreted and thus have empirical validity. Whether called conventionally "sociology" or "political science," the intellectual structure stands apart from both terms. Sociology is the social science that has perhaps the widest generality, yet much of its value derives from achievements in areas conventionally called political science, economics, and anthropology. (And there are people called sociologists who are really engaged in the psychological enterprise.)

Thus the discussion above of interdisciplinary efforts among primitive disciplines should not be considered a stricture. The disciplines of *social* science are all, finally, concerned with the nature and consequences of aggregate behavior of human beings, whether it takes place in an arena defined as a market place, a polity, a kinship network, or a community. The transfer of guiding metaphors from one realm of discourse to another, one social subject matter to another, can only be useful—it increases alternatives and therefore counteracts our collective tendency toward unimaginative empiricism.

[14]

RESEARCH DESIGN
AND OPERATIONALISM

Research is the exploration through experience of relations between our interpretations of the past and the ongoing nature of things. At one pole of the process lies our conceptual scheme, at another, our observations. In Bentley's terms, our tools are the human senses and the human languages, no matter how elaborate their extensions. The great X-ray telescope with an acre of surface is only an extension in range and precision of the human eye, the battery of digital computers an extension of our ability to use the languages of mathematics. They are the present incarnation of the Sumerian priests who saw stars in their courses and described them by geometrical patterns. The procedure is to look and formulate in language.

But the link between observation and formulation is one of the most difficult and crucial in the scientific enterprises. It is the process of interpreting our theory or, as some say, of "operationalizing our concepts." Our creations in the world of possibility must be fitted to the world of probability; in Kant's epigram, "Concepts without percepts are empty." It is also the process of relating our observations to theory; to finish the epigram, "Percepts without concepts are blind." As we have noted, they are both aspects of our ongoing experience, yet their proper relation in scientific research is a major hurdle for any theoretical formulation.

How do we relate a theory of stratification, of classes of people having a "vertical" relationship to each other, to the world we see? What we see is a loose collection of people moving, acting, interacting, but certainly not in the framework of a giant pyramid, the common metaphor. And what is the observation corresponding to "solidarity," "*anomie*," or even "social attitude"? This last is one of the most common explanatory terms for social action; in our everyday life and in the discipline of social psychology it is ubiquitous. What does it mean? "A tendency to act in a certain way," the textbooks may tell us. How shall we measure tendency? LaPiere, in a famous experiment, often unheeded, tried to do it. He wrote to a large number of hotel keepers, asking them for reservations, adding that one of his party would be an Oriental. He was refused reservations. But when he appeared with his party (including the Oriental), he was given accommodations in nearly all cases. What did the measure of "attitude" mean with respect to the social action it implied? Is "attitude" simply a fifth wheel on the automobile, rotating with the others? Is it, then, measurable?

During the 1930's, when social scientists took more and more seriously the Pythagorean dictum to measure, they began to discover how difficult it was. Their concepts did not seem to imply measurable qualities, while what could be measured did not seem to imply their concepts. It was under such circumstances that an irrational revolt occurred. I refer to the vogue of sociologic operationalism, a strategy for avoiding the problems and going on with the enterprise.

Percy Bridgman, an experimental physicist, first used the term. In trying to describe what a scientist does, he emphasized a point Langer makes: a scientist works, not with objects *per se,* but with *indicators* of hypothesized relationships. This led him to interpret his work in terms of his behavior as an experimentalist; thus he emphasized his operations in the laboratory, not his conceptualization of physical theory shared with other physicists. At an extreme, he suggested that a concept "means" a set of operations. But, as Bentley points out, "operation" is not a simple concept.

Operation is thus experience with empirical emphasis, but it is not at all the ancient and absurd "passive" receptivity assigned in theory to fictive "senses," nor does it consist of the equally ancient and absurd isolations of fragmentary experiences alleged to be "facts." What Bridgman put to work in the laboratory was not a robot; neither was it a medicine-man; it was the physicist at work with his hands—himself a phase of the ongoing natural process. He put him there with the clear-eyed recognition that where hands are at work, there head is at work also. . . ."

Science was described by Bridgman as human activity. Because he was most interested in experimental work, however, he tended to pay little attention to what we have called symbolic transformation. In Bentley's words, Bridgman had "a *concept* of an operation but only a *notion* of a concept." Thus Bridgman seemed to say that the concept *is* the operation. Later he clarified his position by emphasizing conceptualization as part of the entire operation.

Social scientists, bedeviled by the hiatus between concepts and measurement, sometimes vulgarized Bridgman's position. Thus the people working with intelligence tests, asked what they measured, could reply "intelligence"; pressed further, they could say that "intelligence is what the test measures." Of course this position is not very useful and in practice the original folk notion of intelligence crept back in; uncontrolled by theoretical specification it was the true meaning of "what the test measures." Many have suffered from this vulgar use of "operationalism" in respect to intelligence.

Physicists could be led to Bridgman's position in an extreme form because they worked within a clear and elaborate theoretical structure. Their basic metaphor is that of mathematics and, as we have seen, a mathematics so elaborated that one can derive the value of one physical function from the mathematical relations with others: What is density? It is a relationship between volume and weight, as each of these is a relationship between the two remaining terms. In this sense, operational definitions demand the clearly specified relationships of other terms in a closed system.

But the poor sociologist is in no such situation when he attempts to measure "social status." He can develop a "Living Room Scale," based upon the material objects in a room (you win 20 points for an oil painting, lose 5 if you have an alarm clock); he can even discover that it correlates with income; but he cannot tell you that "status" is what the scale measures. Living room furnishings do not yield a number that relates to others as density does. The futility of "operationalism" in social science stems from the difficulties in measurement and the lack of relational laws that follow—the very problem it was once hoped "operationalism" would solve.

Indeed, operationalism stands the problem on its head. Our measures of the world take their significance from our laws and hypotheses about the phenomena measured. Measurement means what the concept specifies, or it means anything at all and therefore nothing at all. To be sure it may only approximate the measurement of theoretically specified attributes; indeed, empirical research in primitive science tests *both* concept and theory. Ideally we move from gross approximations of measurement to better ones, and in the process our concepts become more sharply defined; our theory approaches interpretation as our measurements approximate the values they should take in terms of theory.

There is still the major insight of Bridgman to keep in mind. All data may be regarded as *indicators* of variables specified in theory. Then the value of the particular indicator emerges in its relations with others—the only way to assess the utility of a measurement. The operation of measurement is highly contingent.

A large part of social science research consists of studying the invariants in given types of situations that occur without the aid of the scientist. One might call this the "natural experimental" method, for it is simply part of the ongoing process of the world. From it one tries to isolate variables that taken together account for some specific event. Thus we can compare four communities ranging from a modern city to a tribal village, as Redfield did in the Yucatán, and try to spell out the differences as a "folk to urban" continuum resulting from the process called "urbanization." One can study a given class of people and compare them with others and, as Cressey did, compare them with what they have been in order to infer the processes that changed them. We can compare through time, as in history or the study of social change, and over space, as in cross-cultural studies of child-rearing or alcoholism.

But such a natural experimental approach leads to difficulties. In the first place, *too much happens*. There are so many possible invariants in any given set of social behaviors that one may be the dupe of limited observation. Further, this complexity may not only lead us to overestimate the adequacy of our theory; it may also lead to the reverse. Strong relationships may be blurred by "lurking variables." For several elections there has been a close relationship in the states of the old Confederacy between the proportion of the population that is Negro and the Republican vote: the more Negroes the more Republican votes. But this results, not from the Republicanism of Negroes, but from the correlation between Negro population, plantation organization of agriculture and, finally, white racism. When Negro and white votes were separated, Negroes were found to have voted Democratic in much greater proportions.

Here we have the clue to a means of handling the multiplicity of relevant or possibly relevant "third variables." We try to control such variations symbolically, "factoring out" the influence of irrelevant variables. At its simplest, this is a matter of partialing by the third variable: we separate by race to discover the true relationship between Negroes and Republican voting. This is still the preferable way but frequently there are not enough cases to do so, and mathematicians have devised ingenious schemes for estimating the weight other variables have and thereby eliminating it "in principle," controlling for it symbolically.

But there are other drawbacks. Most of our social theory is stated in terms of invariant sequence in time, yet most of the research is at one point in time ("cross sectional" as it is sometimes called). How does one test propositions about processes at one point in time? It is possible only by making inferences about the order in time of past processes through examining their traces in the present. Such inferential chains should be no longer than is absolutely necessary, for they make our very indicators problematic. (We may find such chains collapsing of their own weight when we reconstruct infancy from the recall of middle-aged men.) Ideally, observation is needed before, during, and after change; usually it is only feasible after the fact.

It is for these reasons that social scientists are envious of the control which the laboratory scientist has over the circumstances of the events he studies. And an increasing number of social scientists do emphasize the creation of experimental situations. Following Kurt Lewin and his associates, many now work with *created* groups—small groups of subjects whose behavior is manipulated in such a way as to exhibit only those variables of interest to the investigator. Lewin tested some propositions about the effects of different group structure on behavior *in extremis* by creating the structure and the threat (a mock fire while the groups were in a locked room). In short, Lewin exercised physical and social control where others had used symbolic control.

It is also possible to approximate adequate control through the use of policy-connected research. Social scientists working with a detention home for girls were able to assign girls to cabins according to previously developed theories of group structure and, through observing their behavior, to test derived hypotheses. With even less power, however, the use of existing social structures can still improve the scientist's control: if he can establish the state before a given event, the nature of the event, and the consequence, he can begin to spell out invariant sequence. The prediction of parole behavior is an example of such research.

We have already mentioned the development of simulated social situations as research tools (chapter 12). Here the simulation, whether we deal with "sociodrama," "psychodrama," or "game playing" (and the boundaries are not very sharp), is an effort so to involve an individual in an immediate, contrived situation, that he will behave in it as though it were

"real." Thus we can study the responses of interacting diplo-
mats through a game not altogether unlike poker, or we can
study the political behavior of union leaders through a "sociodrama" in which they interview a person playing the role of
candidate for political office with a view to endorsing or
rejecting him.

There are grave limits to the development of experimental
social science. First, there are the limits imposed by law and
morality on the kinds of behavior that can be produced;
suicide, narcotics addiction, and other actions frowned upon
in the society are not feasible. Then there is the problem of
generalization—how far can the stripped-down world of the
laboratory, surrounded by one-way screens and telescoped in
time, be considered analogous to a looser and sloppier world
outside? This question leads to a related limitation: Can
the massive events important in human history be simulated?
Can we simulate diplomacy under the threat of thermonuclear warfare?

But such efforts are important. They grow out of the intrinsic difficulty of specification that attends our studying society through mere observation. The effort is to improve the
specificity of our variables and thus their measurement, leading toward the creation of truly relational laws. And it may
be that the games men play in the outside world are in
essence isomorphic with many aspects of the games they play
in the laboratories of the social scientists.

THE LOGIC OF EXPLORATION AND
THE LOGIC OF VERIFICATION

It is useful to consider the processes by which we formulate
theory and attendant hypotheses separately from the ways in
which we test them. Studies of methods in the social sciences
typically devote most attention to hypothesis testing, at the
expense of hypothesis formulation. Since much, if not most,
social research is really exploratory in character, this leads

to a certain confusion. It is not clarified by emphasizing the empirical nature of hypothesis testing, for either kind of inquiry may be empirical.

In exploration we create, through experience and reflections upon it, new laws-as-hypotheses, new theories to explain them. We isolate a select set of events that concretizes the kind of problem that interests us; if we are interested in political decisions, we take not a sample of the universe of voters, but a sample of those we believe to make decisions. The emphasis is not upon generalizing to a universe but on finding and understanding the object in question.

Of course we begin exploration with a frame of reference, however vague and unarticulated, with which to define the event. Such a framework is sometimes called a "heuristic" theory or assumption; its value depends upon the consequences of using it. Like certain terms in mathematics, it may slip completely out of the argument by the time we are finished; it is a steppingstone. It serves the purpose of highlighting a kind of relevance and suppressing others. Thus, it is doubtful that Freud believed all failures of memory were determined by his psychodynamics, or Marx that all history is determined by relationships to the means of production, but their intellectual accomplishments justified the assumptions and left others the problem of qualifying them. The heuristic or, as Blumer puts it, the "sensitizing" concept is inescapably part of theory construction.

One of the major ways of exploring social situations is through interacting with the protagonists. Whether one is a participant observer or an observing participant, his chances of intuiting the rationale of behavior are increased by playing a part in the game. Through his imaginings of the imaginations of others he gains awareness of their expectations, learning like any participant, but analyzing in another frame of reference. This kind of understanding (*verstehen,* Max Weber termed it) , is an intense and realistic effort to see the situation from the point of view of the actors in it. It may lead to a conviction on the part of the social scientist that he has explained the event; this esthetic proof is, of course, no better and no worse than that of the other people who work in a machine shop, play in a jazz band, or ride in police prowl cars. In short, we cannot substitute the logic of exploration for verification, however certain we feel.

But we can go far in editing theory, in seeing what does *not* follow as it should. And in the process one frequently learns aspects of the situation unimaginable before empirical experience of it. ("There are more things on Heaven and Earth . . .") Frequently the most valuable part of a research enterprise is the thing we find accidentally rather than the thing we assumed we would find. This process of discovery by inadvertency has been dubbed "serendipity" by Merton, in reference to the three princes of Serendip who followed the same logic of exploration.

It sometimes happens that one thing leads to another in a very profitable fashion. Thus in studying representation of Negroes in labor unions, I assumed that the relative proportion of Negroes in the ascending offices (steward to executive board member to full-time staff) would measure their internal acceptance and influence. I discovered, to my chagrin, that one of the most reactionary and "morally" suspect locals had a very high proportion of Negro stewards. But I found they were chosen because the union did not want its members to initiate action on the job, and Negro members, fearing for their livelihoods in a discriminatory situation, were much more compliant than others. Here union office was an indicator of organizational weakness in the Negro membership. This finding turned my attention to the complex but inescapable problem of variation in the control system of the local, for the very significance of my indicator depended upon it.

Thus in the enterprise of exploration we keep our theory fluid. It can be changed to fit the discovered facts and we can change the categories of facts we are interested in as relationships become clearer to us. The result of exploratory research is a network of meaning, however incomplete and tenuously supported, constructed after the fact to fit the observed events.

It should lead to a more elaborate theory, to more, and more precisely defined, hypotheses.

In verification we are concerned with the generality of the laws we hypothesized. We want to know if they hold over time, in space, in a range of analogous situations. These questions cannot be answered through the exploratory research that resulted in our original hypotheses; such research explains all after the fact, but may predict nothing. The reason is that theory in exploratory research has been expressly designed to account for the events studied; it will work for further events only if the first event selected was adequately representative of the class of events. Consider the unhappy fate of the research documenting discrimination through studying the unequal representation of Jews on the society page of the metropolitan daily: the Sunday newspaper was the one studied and the disproportionate coverage resulted, not from prejudice, but from the fact that the previous day's happenings occurred on the Jewish Sabbath.

When one tailors theory to fit the facts of the case he is always vulnerable to idiosyncrasy in that case. The same holds when one tailors the facts to fit theory. Proof by example is thus suspect whether the example led to the construction of theory or theory led one to hunt down the example. A major aim of verificatory research is a statement of the classes of events to which the theory applies in an unambiguous fashion.

Having formulated a theory of relations among events classified by our abstractions, we design a set of new observations controlled by certain rules. First we choose our data as indicators of the variables stated in our laws; this is very difficult, for a given indicator may indicate many things, and, contrariwise, many different indicators may point to the same theoretical aspect of the subject. In studying social stratification we often use occupation, education, and income as indicators of "socioeconomic class." Each of these attributes is related to many aspects of a person's social life, and all of them to "social class" in the sense of one's share in power, prestige, and pelf. A rigorous selection of an indicator must

emphasize the precise nature of the relata which the laws indicate. (One reason for the crudeness in measures of socioeconomic class lies in the looseness of the laws usually tested.)
Frequently we cannot select an indicator with any degree of
rigor without first analyzing the general statement of the law
into much more precise variations; the unanalyzed abstraction
is a handicap to precise measurement. But if our generalization is "molar" we may be content with crude and approximate measures; occupation, education, or income may do
equally well for indicators of gross inequalities in social per-
quisites.

Using the indicators then as descriptive law, we select a
new set of events for observation. Ideally they will be absolutely independent of those that, in our exploration, gave
rise to the laws we are testing; in this way we escape the predicament described above. And ideally the events selected will
be absolutely unbiased with respect to any confounding variable: they will be a random sample of a class of events. (The
latter is often impossible, so many-dimensional is social life.
Thus if one wishes to compare rural and urban ways of life,
he will have to accept the fact that they differ on many variables that may be irrelevant to his interests, including socioeconomic class. We are frequently forced to control through
partialing and other techniques.)

The new set of observations is then examined in the light
of the theory investigated and its derived hypotheses. If these
are useful, they imply patterns that the new observations
should manifest. They range in rigor from associations "unlikely to occur by random variation" to "specific degrees of
association" to "invariant association." (The rigor with which
one can state the hypotheses will be, of course, dependent
upon the adequacy of measurement and the existence of
mathematical laws.)

A careful comparison of the findings with the hypotheses is
a verification if the laws previously discovered also describe
the new sample. The congruence of data with theory may be
measured point for point; the *power* of the theory is something else. It is manifest in the degrees of association among

attributes, the amount of the "variance" of social behavior accounted for by—for instance—indicators of socioeconomic class. Then too, recalling the metaphor of the map, we can say the more detailed the theoretical map, the more hypothetical checkpoints it affords for testing its congruence with the events observed and, if this works out, the more powerful the verification of theory.

Most theories in social science result in statistical laws, laws stating the probabilities of association. Such laws assume less than a strict one-to-one relationship among items in a class but an invariant degree of relationship among classes. Thus there will usually be "negative cases," in which the relationship does not hold. Such negative cases are then the starting point for new exploratory analysis; we may be led to redefine the class of events, to redefine our indicators, or to revise our statement of the relationship. Such revision aims to bring theory closer to the data, to increase its empirical power. Then it must be tested, in its turn, with new samples.

The effort at verification of theory does not at all foreclose further exploration. Indeed, a major aim is to increase the specificity of the laws by redefinitions and by greater articulation of theory. A statement that two items are related may, in the hypothetical form, only specify the degree as "unlikely to occur by chance"; the empirical findings, however, may lead to a statement of "specific degrees of association." This last becomes a hypothesized mathematical law, to be validated in further research.

Indeed, the common approach to social research uses a *combined* strategy. The subjects studied are of interest in common-sense terms and more careful description is useful if only as a check on common-sense assumptions and as a source of new puzzles for theory. But the data are also chosen as tests of hypotheses derived from theory; they are used to support, negate, or modify theory. And through the analysis of negative cases, through that happy accident called serendipity, they often result in the construction of new theory, new hypotheses, to be tested the next time around.

Lazarsfield and his associates carried out a massive election study that illustrates this approach. They studied a sample of voters who were interviewed and reinterviewed at theoretically significant times during the campaign. Their aim was to assess the importance of the mass media (radio, newspapers, periodicals) in determining the outcome of presidential elections, but they also gathered a wide range of data on social background and informal communication. To the surprise of many they found the media to be singularly ineffective at changing the vote. (This result alone was worth the work.) But more important, they found unexpected solace in the very strong relationships among several social background characteristics and voting; they were princes of Serendip, initiating the dominant line of inquiry in voting studies for the next two decades.

Their descriptive findings were also of value. Among others, the movement of the electorate from a normal distribution of opinion to a highly polarized one as the election approaches and the tendency of the truly "independent" voter to withdraw from political discourse and the ballot are important additions to knowledge.

Yet the value of the study did not stop with these. The sociologists had noticed that, although the media did not seem to communicate well or effect changes, there was a class of citizens extremely receptive to them and (though the data were only impressionistic) they seemed to transmit messages from the media to others who did not attend radio or newspaper. Thus the "two-step communication flow," from media to opinion leader to followers, was discovered. It led to the study of opinion leadership, the variation by social class in direction of influence, the variation by "issue field," and other topics. Then Merton, studying opinion leadership in a small city, was struck by the existence of two quite different and nonoverlapping classes of opinion leaders—the "localites," and the "cosmopolites," those whose careers and interests were local, as against those interested in the nation and the world. He related this to their role in organization and the scale of the organizational nexus they worked in. This in turn led to other studies of social space and psychological horizons.

In this example we can see the combined strategy at its best. Theory and hypothesis testing, careful description of events (even though in common-sense terms), and the formulation of new theories fruitful of testable hypotheses, combine in the given inquiry. The critical distinction between exploration and verification is that between the formulation of hypotheses and their testing—the evidence for the generality of a law.

But what are the limits of generalization in the social sciences? In one sense we cannot answer on a *priori* grounds; it is an empirical question. But we can note the laws that have been successful and see several types. There are certainly laws that work within a given culture but are still culture-bound; such are the laws of kinship, which anthropologists have documented carefully for many years. There are also laws that are society-bound, which hold with a high degree of consistency within a society though one reaches their limits as he moves to very dissimilar societies. And, a composite, there is the "time" limit (actually, societies are quite different social forms over time), which allows us to state invariant associations for feudal society that are quite irrelevant today.

But the most general laws are those that refer to conditions not affected by a given set of limits. They are analytical and will some day perhaps be expressed in a "created language" that, avoiding the culture-bound vocabularies we use today, will emphasize the similar variables that operate in all societies. These would appear to be laws of socialization by which biological individuals become members of groups and laws of organization by which groups emerge, maintain themselves, change, and die. It seems likely that all laws holding for very simple societies will hold for complex, large-scale ones, though the reverse would probably not be true. There are such things as emergent social forms, as there are emergent ideas in the individual and emergent culture patterns in the collective.

As for understanding human history, it seems obvious that we can analyze parts of it in terms of social scientific laws. We can explain the relationships between culture and fertility rates, slavery and kinship systems, political power and the caste system. But this does not necessarily mean we can control or even, except within narrow limits, predict human history. We must understand broad configurations of forces through analyzing from laws discovered in miniature, in the data accessible to us. And though we will learn more about the conditions for emergence, we had best keep in mind the multitudinous variables and the complexities of their combinations, and go slowly in predicting exactly *what* will emerge in human symbolization.

Finally, we might note the limits of human history. It is the story of one species on one small planet—perhaps quite idiosyncratic, perhaps not. All that we know, as the source of the "facts" that are puzzles for social science, is the one story.

[IV]

SOCIAL SCIENCE AND VALUES

[15]

NORMATIVE THEORY
AND EMPIRICAL THEORY

At the meetings of the International Sociological Association in 1962 a plenary session was held jointly with the American Sociological Association. The subject was social science and the developing nations and in this circumstance an interesting confrontation came about.

A parade of social scientists from the new nations (the countries called, depending upon your optimism, "underdeveloped" or "developing") crossed the podium. Social scientists of all colors and nationalities spoke to one point: What can social science do for our nation? How can we achieve our goals? These men were mostly from socialist countries and some were from the communist bloc. Underlying their speeches was a common assumption: social science theory fails us when it does not focus upon our pressing problems.

A distinguished American sociologist spoke last. His presentation was clear and, in the language of an introductory methods class, he argued the absolute necessity for an unbiased social science. Social science must be value-free; it cannot be tied to the chariot of any given ideology or national goal. If it is it becomes not science but apologetics. The answer was that his own social science, in accepting the terms of his society, was an apologetics; in failing to ask the major questions it accepted the American *status quo*.

Here was not a dialogue but a classical case of two parties talking past one another. The American's argument for a purely empirical science without concern for consequences seemed hypocritical to the men of the new nations; their argument for a sociology *engagé* seemed to him a juvenile dissimulation on the part of men who neither understood sociology nor intended to help create it. Practicing a discipline only recently emerged from frantic concern with social amelioration at the expense of empirical research and proof, the American saw the "new men" as counseling regression to prescientific thought.

Let us forget for the moment who was right or admirable in the interchange. What seems more to the point is the fact that they were not addressing the same question at all. Both parties spoke of "social science theory" but they did not have the same referent in mind. The Marxists meant a teleological theory, a purposive approach to the world resting on the intent to intervene in and change its course; the American meant an empirical theory that described the world as it is. Both usages are correct, for the concept of "theory" is quite neutral with respect to the nature of the spatio-temporal realm. It is a formulation of experience in terms of concepts; that experience may vary from *what is* to *what ought to be*.

This conflict is reflected in the origins of social thought and social science as we know it. In the thought systems of the classical civilizations one wished to know the *proper* approach to reality, the *correct* relations to the nature of things. Confucius, Lao Tse, and Guatama Buddha were not the only thinkers to emphasize the teleological; the Greeks also mixed what is and what ought to be in their thinking. Aristotle explained biology and society in terms of things striving for their "proper form," for explanation was given in a result that was either adequate or pathological.

But the origins of a powerful empirical science lay in the separation of these two realms. While Newton may have considered his work in theology as his most important achievement, it is notable that he did not mix it with his physical theory. He may have believed in witchcraft, but there are no pixies in the workings of the "Newtonian world machine." So in the beginnings of social science it was necessary to separate what is from what is wanted. Dante treated the state as an ideal, in true Aristotelian fashion, but Machiavelli treated it empirically: What must a Prince do to seize and keep power?

Yet the impulse to see social life in terms of what should be continues to be a *leitmotif* in the thought of social scientists. Even Comte, while heralding the scientific as successor to the religious and metaphysical stages, was heavily invested in purpose, going so far as to design a "scientific" religion. And the powerful global theories of human behavior propounded by Marx and Freud were saturated with value judgments. Though Marx attempted a rigorous determinism, the hortatory strain is ubiquitous: one must help History bring to birth the revolution. Though Freud thought in a disciplined way of the human animal and its nervous system, the pathological bias of the practitioner was usually evident; neurosis was illness and one must cure the sick.

Such ambiguities continue unabated in the application of social science to society. Political scientists are dedicated, among other things, to the good state—whether defined as socialism, capitalist democracy, or what not. They build an industry upon the supposed requirements for "good citizenship," including, in the United States, participation in a two-party system in which the parties are indistinguishable. Social workers are interested in their cases only as problems to be "solved"; clinical psychologists continue to judge their theories by whether the ministrations produce "cures"; economists are concerned with making the economy "work." Thus the Marxist critique of American social science has some validity; as it focuses upon maintaining a given system it is tacitly committed to that system.

The result is confusion. On the one hand we have views of what should be inhibiting investigation of what is. Whether we deal with political scientists prescribing a new government for a metropolitan area, or socialists prescribing a new society, the result is the same: an arrogant assumption that one understands existing society without investigating it, that the meaning of that society will only be manifest in what it becomes. At an extreme, this leads to a definition of everything in the present that inhibits your ideal as pathological. Thus general theories and the minute particulars alike are vitiated; the former become weapons, the latter signs of an imminent transformation of the world.

At the other extreme an equally dangerous strategy emerges. One's belief as to what exists is translated into his estimate of what should be: scientific theory masquerades as normative theory. So the practitioner of public administration theory believes he advocates the scientific solution to problems of equity, redistribution of income, and other major issues in the society; the physician prescribes the scientific solution to drug use or alcoholism; the psychologist solves, scientifically, problems of marriage.

We see the conflict most clearly in the Marxist movements at the turn of the century. Those who followed Marx were bent upon proselytizing and acting as midwives of the Revolution. But Marx's theory was deterministic and this contradiction did not escape the eyes of others; the "revisionists" said, in effect: If it is inevitable it must emerge anyway, so why strain yourself? A consistent determinism has no room for voluntarism; the reverse seems also to hold. As a scientist Marx was a determinist, as a citizen a voluntarist.

The fault lies not in Marx, but in the nature of our discourse. When we find two modes of thought inextricably involved in a problem yet logically contradictory, it is imperative that we separate them in our analysis. Naming them is a beginning; we hope it may lead toward taming them. For this reason let us assume two different modes, empirical theory and normative theory. Let empirical theory refer to the study of fact that has a validity quite independent of our wishes— the laws of gravity will do. Then let normative theory refer to our study of desirable futures, quite dependent upon our wishes—our notions of right conduct, the just state, the good society, will do. It is clear the two are separate, but it is certain that they meet in our beliefs and actions.

NORTHROP'S EFFORTS

F. S. C. Northrop has attempted to clarify the matter through his analysis of normative theory. His is a serious effort, and it can be taken as representative of many other attempts. He begins with the proposition that in social theory we often cannot ignore normative theory, because that is precisely what the problems are about. Any solution must then be a normative solution.

Normative theory is synthetic, it refers to the meeting of concept and sense data in our experience, and in this way it is empirical. But it is quite obviously not descriptive of empirical reality. Indeed, if we use this approach we end up with the Panglossian position: all is for the best in the best of all possible worlds. (Or, at another level, might makes right.) If, however, we disregard the empirical description of the world and construct normative theory by other principles, our theory has no empirical validity at all. There are too many alternative theories that may be freely proposed and have equal validity, in which case none has any.

Northrop believes he has found a solution by grounding normative theory in empirical descriptive theory. Go, he says, to the postulates behind the philosophy of a culture—for a culture can be seen as a logical system of norms—and test them by their congruence with the postulates behind natural science. Does the culture assume that the biological individual evolves, regardless of human association, to produce something recognizably human in behavior? We know it is not so. Is it assumed that genetics determines culture? We know it is not so.

In brief, those aspects of culture congruent with empirical descriptive theory are better because they integrate theories of what ought to be. In doing so they improve the practical probabilities of achieving the norms, as they edit out confusion and hypocrisy from the normative system. With this approach we should be able to construct larger frameworks that would include a wide variety of cultures congruent with nature and exclude those cultural complexes in serious contradiction with nature, the postulates of science. Thus the product would be a scientific theory of normative adequacy.

The solution is attractive, particularly so for a secular culture in which many identify with the achievements of science. Yet in terms of Northrop's effort, it will not do. One can accept it if he wishes, and reject it likewise; it has no coercive power either empirically or logically. Thus it is a-scientific.

We are creatures of our culture and from it derive our moral bases for judgment. Yet cultures do not require logical articulation in order to maintain this moral system; as we have seen earlier (chapter 5), the most absurd contradictions can be held by the same people with little evidence of strain. It seems that Northrop assumes a philosophical determinism, neglecting to see the culture as completed only in the activities of the society. Much of the philosophical discontinuity and contradiction in a culture reflects tensions, lags, conflicts—instability in human relations, not logical naïveté.

Northrop assumes a natural man, but there is no natural man, no man without culture. This is one of the most general and well-proved findings of social science. The Greeks were correct; man without his social group is something less than human. Yet the man we do observe, and describe in precise empirical terms, whose behavior we account for by relational laws, is a man whose nature is perfectly congruent with the entire range of cultures that have existed. We cannot even propound functional necessities that will determine cultural limits; there are too many negative cases.

The Kaingaing of Brazil developed a culture system resulting in progressive annihilation of the society through the cult of force and blood-revenge. At a more civil level, consider the Shakers, a utopian cult in the United States who abjured procreation. It did no good to tell them they were violating a functional prerequisite; they did not care if the entire community disappeared (as it did). Culture may be seen as an organization of desire and desire is limited only in a very broad way by reality as perceived by the social scientist.

We cannot prove a normative theory by empirical evidence and therefore science cannot produce a required normative theory. What Northrop (and others of his persuasion) is really proposing is that assumptions about the desirable be derived from assumptions about empirical inquiry. Should he succeed, his achievement would be great; it would still be a matter of persuasion and not that coercion of evidence which gives scientific proof.

For a "logical proof of the good," that aim of ethics, has very rigorous empirical prerequisites. The parties to the argument must, at the most general level, share the same postulates; they must also agree upon logic as a criterion and upon the nature of that logic. ("Common sense" will not do—it varies too widely in method.) But as we have seen, the very basis of science as an enterprise is a set of postulates that cannot be proved, that must indeed be freely accepted, and are in principle results of reversible decisions.

Thus Northrop's empirical approach to normative theory is itself one more normative theory. He says: If you wish the beneficial results of editing normative theory by empirical theory, then you must proceed in the following manner. The corollary is: If not, not.

We may raise the question whether it is even useful to call normative assumptions and propositions "theory." Perhaps it is too pretentious, implying as it does order in the postulates, and articulation and consistency in the derived propositions and applications. Is normative theory in any sense comparable to empirical theory? Can we transfer rules from one to the other? Do they relate meaningfully?

Lévi-Strauss suggests that normative theories, whether the "dialectic" of Marx or the "totemism" of Australian tribes, are essentially *bricolage*. That is, they are a type of construction, from odds and ends and artifacts that lie at hand, of a structure whose guiding principles are as much esthetic as anything else. They are a way of integrating a view of the world for the purpose of action, including such acts as explanation to the curious and justification to the inquisitorial. Their logic is as much presentational as discursive—symbols evoke, and their joint evocations create an ambiance rather like the clash of overtones from carillons played rapidly.

Yet their referents are, at least in part, quite empirical. Thus we might see a normative theory as a hypothesis about what we will find in our experience of the world. Further, the grand normative theory—the utopia, the chiliastic vision— might be conceived as a hypothetical statement of social change. If such and so were done then such and so would result. The deeper hypothesis is that in the result would lie an achievement of value. In this sense, science can and does greatly limit the logical relevance of some normative theories. And since these are, in fact, controlled and reversible in the light of their implications, there is a continual dialectic between the normative and the empirical theories.

But unlike science, normative theories do not refer to judgments upon which universal agreement is possible. Since this is so, they are not falsifiable: thus they cannot be true. Like works of art, they are more or less adequate in the view of the participant or critic (see chapter 8). But since they are not falsifiable they can have no logical "truth value." They must remain—no matter how congruent they are with the empirical scientific view of human experience, no matter how clear and well articulated their "theology"—matters of faith and, finally, matters of choice.

Yet much of the direction of social inquiry seems to be influenced, if not determined, by normative theory. Whether it be the vast questions of social philosophy that led Marx to create his *bricolage* (from classical economics, evolutionary theory, and socialist ardor), or the pressing questions of social reform and amelioration, which in America resulted in studies of welfare, race conflict, and deviation, the intense concern with matters of value certainly contributed to the efforts. The focus resulted, in each case, in a kind of "tunnel vision" of society—with Marxists underestimating the tenacity of old forms, and some Americans underestimating, as my colleague Arnold Feldman puts it, the amount of "violence and volatility" that persists in the most stable and complacent society.

In empirical fact, then, the two modes of thought interact intimately, with both social science and social ideology as their progeny. Analytically they are quite different operations and should not be confused. We might speculate as to why men have been so concerned, as is Northrop, with relating them more organically. The answer seems to be a desire to ground moral choice in scientific certainty—and so to escape the terrible gamble of freedom. But to do so is to escape politics and move toward a rule by philosophers and scientists (or, more realistically, bureaucrats more or less indoctrinated by them).

And it is in the areas of policy-making that the interaction between normative and empirical theory is most critical. All the ambiguities we have noted, all the arguments for "the one right way," and all the implicit contradictions, come to play in the evolution of social policy. Let us consider some specimen cases and ask: What can social science do for social policy? as well as the companion: What can social policy do for social science?

[16]

SOCIAL SCIENCE
AND SOCIAL POLICY

Social science is, in a profound sense, the business of creating social fact. That fact may be crude and erroneous but it is finally a necessity for any public policy; since it is a basis for important policy decisions it is a critical input into human destiny. William the Conqueror relied upon that census reported in the Domesday Book for data useful in exploiting his new possession; the United States relies upon the estimates and interpretation of Kremlinologists, experts on Russia, in making major foreign policy decisions. It does no good to protest that these facts are not solid; they have solid consequences in the destiny of nations.

To be sure, we do not often consider the matter in this light. Our everyday discourse assumes a simple "finding of facts," which lie out there in the world. Facts are those assumed existential realities of stability and change underlying the belief that a problem exists as well as that effort to intervene in the flow of things we term policy. Thus social action is always dependent upon such regularities. Since this is the case, an early contribution of social science to policy lies in introducing "data quality control" to improve the accuracy of social fact. If a decision to intervene in a neighbor's revolution depends upon whether it is defined as a civil war or an invasion by enemy forces, no amount of argument can substitute for accurate data. (Assuming, of course, that one has an adequate definition of civil war versus invasion.)

Much of what is taken for social fact is, when measured by the standards discussed earlier, weak indeed. Take the case for marijuana control. It rests upon two assumptions: that marijuana is a dangerous, addictive drug, driving people mad; and that the way to prevent the use of drugs is to outlaw them. Both are patently false; both were built into a policy of control.

Marijuana is made from Indian hemp, a crop grown commercially in this country for many decades. In the years before it was outlawed, laborers in the harvest fields of Indiana smoked it as they gathered the crop; to the Mexican-Americans of the Southwest, it was a staple of cheap, mildly euphoric parties. (It is, when legal, much cheaper than alcohol; its suppression may be one more aspect of the class war over vice. In this war the issue is: Whose vice is virtuous?) But a propaganda campaign linking ethnicity, horror at hallucinations, and exaggerated stories of dementia and violence resulted in its suppression. The penalties for selling, owning, and smoking the hemp were made very drastic indeed.

There were a number of predictable results. First, users of marijuana who had been law-abiding citizens were now "vicious criminals." Such was the social fact created. (One creates law-breakers by making a law.) Second, by outlawing the drug the authorities created a market quickly entered by those specialists in illegal products, the organized criminals. This market, protected by legislation, resulted in much higher prices; what had been very cheap became expensive. Third, the organizations selling marijuana often did not want a buyer's use to stop there; marijuana is not addictive so it cannot develop lifetime consumers who will pay any price for the commodity. Consequently some peddlers concentrated on introducing novices to the heavy narcotics that are addictive. Outlawing marijuana placed some of those who used it in a position to interact with the international underworld of narcotics traffic.

Thus the result of the policy to suppress marijuana was the exact opposite of its aims. New customers were introduced to addictive drugs and drug addiction increased thereby.

Whatever one thinks of drug addiction (and judgments vary immensely over time and cultures), the point is that social policies should not produce results exactly opposite from the stated goal. Hospitals should not spread disease, drug control policies should not spread addiction. With defective social fact we cannot have a meaningful debate of public policy, for we all inhabit the same (hallucinatory) symbolic system.

One can see such corrupt social fact as reflecting merely conspiracy on the part of the makers of law. It is sometimes the case, for social facts are weapons and are used as such. More often, however, it reflects an unthinking acceptance of the cliché at hand—and that cliché is usually out of the conventions and moralities of earlier societies where it may even have served as adequate. (One accompaniment of the "disenchantment of the world" is an increasingly higher standard for fact—not a trivial gain.)

Thus older policies with respect to poverty in the United States reflected the ethos of the nineteenth century small farmer and shopkeeper. Since for such folk all had opportunity, poverty was an indication of incompetence and/or immorality. This secular version of the doctrine of predestination only left room for the exercise of the Christian charity complex on the part of the state. With new circumstances, however, as the poor became increasingly unprofitable for the economy as a whole, the "facts" behind poverty were examined in a more empirical way. The resulting treatment of the problem saw poverty as a result of social learning (and not learning), of weakness in the relationship between family and economy, of the position of the aged and the ethnic in American society. Defined in such commonplace concepts of social science, the problem became amenable to action in the same terms.

But the creation of an improved set of facts which are effective in the origin and design of social policy is not an easy matter. To begin with, there are enormous hiatuses in our social science theory and the propositions we can derive from it are often vague and contingent. Lloyd Rodwin has discussed the situation of the British planners in these terms:

The fact is that the town planners' intellectual lines have been overextended: their base needs strengthening; their supplies are limited; they are operating in unknown terrain; and their key personnel are not well enough equipped for many of the problems that lie ahead.

Under such circumstances almost any application of social science is apt to be in some degree "premature," and there is a real danger that it will be oversold. Officials may expect a kind of efficacy impossible without long and careful experimentation.

Two directives seem to follow from this situation. First, it is necessary that more energies be committed to developing and testing basic theories of social science, those powerful generalizations that once discovered illuminate a wide range of situations. And, equally important, it is necessary for the social scientist to speak the truth about the state of the art when commenting on policy issues. To do so he must abnegate the mantle of professional charisma and adopt the role of the craftsman of social fact; this is where his real authority lies. In the process he may be able to educate other social actors to the differences between normative and empirical theory, as well as the variable truth value of the latter. In short, his effectiveness finally depends upon the intellectual comprehension of social science among his audience or clients.

For his social facts are potentially dangerous. He may add to confusion, as his tentative formulations are turned into dogmas. Thus today there is an ongoing and complex debate over the nature of community politics in the United States, yet battle lines are often drawn between "the movement" and an assumed "community power structure" that may be quite imaginary. (In the process one *may* create such a structure.) In a similar fashion, our urban policy is couched in terms of an outgrown metaphor that compares cities to trees, sees neighborhoods as "blighted," and chronicles population change in neighborhoods as "invasion and succession" of different species. The generalizations of the social scientist have a way of turning into social fact some decades after they have been abandoned by the discipline.

Even when theories and tools are adequate, social science may be ignored in favor of the conventional wisdom. Thus the 1964 Republican candidate for the American Presidency relied upon an "invisible conservative majority" that had been rejecting all previous candidates as too liberal. Any competent political scientist could have demonstrated that he was in error; he was not convinced until his campaign was dead. Men of affairs prefer to rely on folk thought and the formulations they learned long ago in the universities of another epoch; as Keynes noted, the "practical" politician is usually obeying the words of some defunct economist. They are not alone in this.

There is a spurious assumption of authority in the conventional wisdom. After all, it probably came from unimpeachable sources, and much of our acceptance of theory is based wholly on authority. And in a simpler society where change moves slowly, folk thought may have been enough for the individual to survive and prosper. Our case is different and for most of our catastrophic issues there are few precedents in the past. Thus willynilly the practical men must ask the social scientists for answers, not because they have them but because somebody has to formulate the situation. Premature application of social science is an inevitable result of cultural complexity and change. At an extreme, the social scientist may be little more than an "uncertainty absorber"—a planner who designs zoning ordinances because somebody must do it, an administrative analyst who designs a school district in a given manner because it must be designed in some fashion.

However rational and specific a policy may be, however congruent with dependable social science, it must still be instituted through a political process of some sort. In that process there is typically confusion between what is desirable and what is possible, the aims of a program and the weight of political power. In the process of bargaining off votes critical parts of an integrated plan may be distorted or omitted, leaving the resulting "package" an unworkable monstrosity. Thus urban renewal, as a program to improve housing, may result in the destruction of hundreds of thousands of dwellings in "slums," but without a new supply of "standard" houses at low cost to replace them, have the unintended effect of raising the price and lowering the quality of housing for the poor. Without new public housing, urban renewal fails, but the goal of public housing is politically unpopular, the slum clearance program popular, and the result is again 180 degrees away from the goal. We destroy the housing of the poor.

Once a program has been accepted politically it still remains only legitimated aspiration until it is organized in the actions of men. Here again, the administrative structure may distort and delete important parts of a whole. Based as it is upon precedent, protocol, antiquated theory, and political adroitness, administration may have the effect of sabotaging the most rational programs. If the theory behind the policy is not understood and accepted by those who implement it they may unwittingly make nonsense of policy; the ward attendants at the psychiatric hospital, in constant attendance on the patients, may effectively define the purpose of the hospital. No matter what psychiatric theories the therapists use, the attendants create the atmosphere and fact of a prison. (Their theories about the causation of mental illness may be the folk notions of possession by demons or moral turpitude, their treatment repression and punishment.)

We tend to exaggerate greatly the rationality of the society and thus our ability to make rational policy. For looking at the whole through time, it is clear that much of the collective results of decisions amounts to inadvertency, with accident, ignorance, and mistake the real demiurges of our histories. Yet underlying our behavior there is obviously a massive order, as in our thoughts and in various degrees in our actions. A continental power grid, space travel, and catastrophic wars require and produce systems for ordering the behavior of men, materials, and messages in fantastic scope and precision.

But it is a partial order. Within a given segment of society there may be a precise fitting of means to ends and highly predictable operations over time, yet the rationality of scattered parts does not mean a comprehensive order for the whole; indeed we may purchase a small order at the price of a greater disorder. Labor unions and management may resolve their conflicts at the price of an unrepresented third party—another firm, another union, consumers of their joint product. To be sure, one can simply describe the society as it exists and call it ordered, but this is not a rationalized order. It is more aptly described as a symbiosis among organizations, with various systems competing, conflicting, flourishing, and dissolving.

The social order is partial for a more profound reason. As we have noted earlier, any given order, rationalized or not, applies only to aspects of the individual; other aspects may be ordered by other norms and belief systems, or they may be practically autonomous with respect to society. Even if we would, we could not participate in an order comparable to that of the social insects; the process of symbolization, the origin of our rationality, is also the origin of our irrational and arational action. Scattered individuals are able to be rational about some aspects of their experience but rationality, interpreted strictly as a self-conscious fitting of means to ends, is probably more rare than is generally believed.

But social science may easily drift into a view of man that assumes him to be much more socially determined in his behavior than is the case. Harsh walls of custom, contract, dominance, and law certainly constrain much of our behavior, but these limits are not impermeable and there is always some slippage in the system of control. If much of our life is spent in what Santayana called "normal madness," unthinking conformity to the social surface of things, some is still spent in questioning limits and devising surfaces more conducive to what we hope for.

THE USES OF SOCIAL SCIENCE

What, then, can social science do for social policy? We have already noted that it can improve social fact—it can help us to achieve whatever ends we have stated in general terms, in the context of specific empirical situations. This endeavor is certainly worth doing, but it is limited; it treats social science as simply instrumental, the social scientist as a "gun for hire." This aim is a far cry from the great ideologists who promulgated a view of history and the future, a place for the individual in a cosmos.

And indeed we can go further. Social scientists have no mandate to prescribe the ends of a society, but they can certainly evaluate those ends against the means at hand. They can demonstrate a range of truth values for policy from the impossible to the likely success. And in the process they can demonstrate the costs of the policy. For though one may be quite unable to put values to such dimensions as esthetic satisfaction and social justice, it is frequently possible to "solve for" these values by calibrating what they would cost in terms of material sacrifice.

They can also indicate kinds of cost that may have escaped the eye of the policy maker. By choosing given means to an end, we are always incurring two sorts of cost. First, we are incurring "opportunity costs," the things we foreclose by choosing a given route to the goal. What have we lost when we adopt rote learning as the best means of inculcating mathematics in young children? Probably the opportunity to interest them in the operations they have memorized. Second, when we choose a means to an end we are incurring costs in the side effects, created like wakes from the sides of a boat. Thus the use of punishment in teaching children (whether in school or at home) has the effect of creating hostility directed against the teacher; he then has two problems, and handling hostility may tax his capacity more than the job of instruction.

In short, cost-accounting social policy in a more inclusive and systematic way requires a broad frame of reference, one that sets the policy problem in a complex social context. This requirement means the social scientist should be able to aid policy formation by using his particular vision to indicate alternative courses of action; his training should result in a point of view free from the intellectual ruts of the specialist at politics, just as his base in another discipline (and usually, organization) frees him from the political pressure that, often unconsciously, makes certain ideas taboo. In short, social scientists, used to a complex view of an interacting society and to treating the given regularities as at least intellectually problematic, may be fertile sources of innovation. They know that it can be done differently, for it has been elsewhere.

The group of social scientists who proposed the guaranteed annual income is a case in point. They demonstrated how little it would cost to see that all citizens had adequate money for subsistence—trivial in terms of the total income of the United States. In reaching the conclusion that this scheme would work, however, they assumed an intellectual tradition that included the knowledge of societies in which work is not so separated from play as in our puritan citadel—societies such as the Trobriand Islands, where men worked without the continual pressure of the threat and the bribe. And at a less esoteric level, they were aware of modern large-scale societies, such as Norway, where the creation of security for all had not caused an attrition of industriousness.

My concern is not to argue for such a policy but to indicate the way social scientists can bring new ideas into a political arena. Whether a policy is made the law of the land is, however, beyond the competence of political scientist or economist to decide. Policy making is *choice* and must remain a choice. Requiring normative theory as well as empirical theory, it rests finally upon the rank order of values, which can and does vary immensely among the citizenry and their representatives. Thus there is no scientific way to determine whether you want a society to support those who are inept and unproductive. Many Americans probably think such a policy immoral, a threat to the very nature of morality. What is the value of such beliefs? That can only be settled through the political process, for there is no means of reaching universal agreement on this kind of fact. Thus politics is absolutely inescapable; in whatever guise, it is the way that we resolve our normative differences.

Social science can, however, improve the level of discourse. By showing the implicit assumptions underlying the arguments, it is often possible to clarify the nature of differences—sometimes they disappear. Intellectual somnambulism is a dangerous thing for governments that increasingly hold the very existence of the world in their hands. One cannot decide by scientific means what is right but he can, frequently, show implications and significances that allow the policy to be better related to reality. It has been said that the British acquired an empire in a fit of absentmindedness—a degrading way to make policy.

Finally, a brief for policy as a resource for social science. We have noted earlier that social policy may approximate the classical experiment if we know what the situation is before action, what the action signifies in a theoretical frame of reference, and what the consequences are. Such research allows us to use the society as a laboratory without confusing normative and empirical thought. But we may go further; if research were systematically built into all action programs it would be possible continually to adjust both the procedures of the action agency and the theories of the social scientist. These latter usually include a time element; continuous monitoring and evaluation of such radical innovations as urban renewal and the efforts to eliminate poverty should allow an increasing specification of theories, increasing understanding of processes, and at the same time a closer fit between means and end, action and goal.

[17]

THE THIRD CULTURE
AND THE SELF-FULFILLING
PROPHECY

Most of history has been carried on by dim and primitive light. Religious dogma, folk thought, the quasi-religious speculations of philosophers, provided what general theory of experience and the world we used. Our empirical knowledge was limited to common sense, lore, and the chroniclers, old men who told the tales of the tribe around the firelight in the evening. To be sure, common sense was organized and handed down through the organizations that carried on the work of the world: farmers told their sons the methods for planting and harvesting and evading taxes, as tax collectors told their new employees what tricks to expect and how to catch the tricksters. But these were, essentially, recipes for action. They were arts, not sciences.

With the great intellectual revolution which exploded in the seventeenth century this state of affairs was changed, radically and probably for good. On many fronts—physics, astronomy, biology, chemistry, geology—men made the world of folklore problematic. They turned the realities of everyday life into intellectual problems to be solved. The triumph of classical mechanics proved the value of the approach; a new and strange world, inexorable in its structure and predictable in its behavior, seemed to be emerging.

Enthusiasts of the new science early attempted to use it in explaining human affairs. Hobbes imagined a physics of political structure from which an applied science of politics could be derived; Comte saw the coming period dominated by science, succeeding the metaphysical and religious periods. The success of these forerunners of social science was less scientific than ideological; they bequeathed major questions but few propositions amenable to scientific test. They did leave a radical intellectual position called, indifferently, scientism, positivism, neopositivism, or latterly behaviorism. It is a position stressing the causal determination of human behavior. This position has two correlates: (1) human behavior is constrained and determined by inescapable conditions that may be understood through laws discoverable in general, applicable to the given case; (2) the way to discover those laws is through the observation of human behavior, the development of hypotheses about patterns found and the testing of hypotheses through new observations.

The new position had no difficulty in finding its enemies. They were devotees of the older tradition called the "classical education," the "liberal education" or the "humanities." Such disciplines tended to stress dramatic evocations of the past, speculations in metaphorical terms about the present, hortatory theories of the future. Abnegating the possibility of a true science of human society, such spokesmen tended to fall into the position of having to prove it impossible. The battleground was, of course, the university: where else are major intellectual issues attacked? Within the university, the major field of conflict was in the humanities.

These latter, defined as everything that was neither true science nor vocational education, witnessed the progressive dissolution of their subject matter. From philosophy emerged psychology; from the philosophy of history came sociology and economics; from the faculty of law came political science; anthropology came from a curious marriage of biology, religion, and philosophy. In general, the development has been in one direction: toward the intellectual position described above, positivism or behaviorism. The break was far from clean, however, for in each of the developing social sciences the hostages to an older tradition were very much alive.

Meanwhile, between the remaining humanities and the behavioral sciences the conflict burned brightly.

The results of this conflict include the development of two
cadres in the world of the intellect. One is made up of ignorant humanists, the other of insensitive scientists. Both per-
petrate confusions of fact and value; neither seems capable of
bridging to a synthesis. Typically, the humanists state moral
and esthetic preferences in the guise of empirical fact; scientists state matters of fact and believe them to be statements
of moral value. But the humanist's appreciation for an artifact has little to do with the conditions of its creation, while
the public-opinion analyst's findings on faith in God have
nothing to do with theology.

Thus the recent polemics concerning the "two cultures"
lead not to a resolution but to a heightening of conflict.
Neither Mr. Snow nor Mr. Leavis demonstrates anything except the sharpness of the separation. The means of integrating
our intellectual world remain as problematic as ever.

AN ALTERNATIVE APPROACH

If we take the world of human experience as a naïve given,
we can see various types of abstraction being derived from it.
Using specific frames of reference, suppressing detail and highlighting forms, human beings process the world as they relate
to it. There are many frames of reference possible—in principle, an infinite range. For everyman we can assume, generally,
the common-sense frame, the "practical vision" of his particular culture. To be sure, that can vary greatly, from an emphasis on *satyagraha* to one on cannibalism, but it will have
commonalities. It will be learned unexamined and tested only
by efficacy (practical and consensual). It changes when change
is practically inescapable. Much of anyone's life is controlled
by such an abstractive frame. But some of everyone's life,
and a great deal of the life of certain specialists, are controlled by other abstractive frames.

Practitioners of the arts use highly developed abstractive frames that highlight the minutest details in terms of the esthetics of form. Their basic touchstone is that "esthetic component" in experience which F. S. C. Northrop has emphasized, and their greatest professional burden is to see their work interpreted in the scientific or didactic mode. Kin to this framework, though far from it in substance, is the view of the moralist: here the precise distinctions of judgment arise from a focus upon what *is* in the light of what he thinks *should be*. But the framework of the scientist stands in sharp distinction to both. Practicing the grim art of determining the ineluctable, a scientist is interested in the esthetic component only as a subject for analysis or a clue to the operational definition. He is interested in the moralist as a subject to be explained and predicted and finds his own method quite blind to the nature of what should be.

None of these particular abstractive frames is required by the immediate experience. In point of fact, they are predictable from one's social learning—whether it be the general culture of the tribe or the common culture of a specialty within the tribe. But they are never completely predictable; whether responsibilities begin in dreams, accidents, slippage of metaphor, or the systematic search for the new, the frame of reference keeps changing. In this lies the possibility of synthesizing the abstract frameworks and creating a viable position for contemporary man.

MAN AS A SUBJECT
FOR ABSTRACTION

One of the ways to think of man is to start with a given objective physical world. Man is the residue. If however the previous discussion seems valid, the more useful approach is to say that "the physical, 'objective' world is one abstraction from our experience." Should we do this, nature is placed within human experience and man squarely in the world.

The objective is everywhere, its determination a pragmatic problem. Thus the world of physics is one possible abstraction from the continuum of individual and collective human experience. On the face of it, it has no more or less utility than the world of the moralist, the artist, or the mystic.

If we take social action as our subject, however, and want to know the hard, inescapable facts of it, how do we define man? We can look at the behavior of a species through time— but that is only one of the abstractive frames we can use. It was Sigmund Freud's. The difficulty with it is that man seems to have the magic art of self-transformation. Trobrianders differ from Viennese; laws that apply to Merovingian kings apply with indifferent results to De Gaulle; birthrates oscillate like heat waves in July. The truth is that the appropriate abstractive framework for looking at man in a scientific way, expecting prediction and putative control, must build in his peculiar symbolic control system. The same facts that differentiate intellectuals by esthetic, moral, and scientific viewpoint—the facts that promise synthesis—must also be accepted by the most behavioral student of human action. As Merton says, men generate self-fulfilling prophecies. To define man is to stipulate his status as a symbolically controlled beast who generates and transforms symbols.

If we understand this, we understand some of the quarrels between the behaviorists and the humanists. The behaviorists, those terrible simplifiers, would like to predict all generation and transformation of symbols—leaving out the likelihood of the emergence of what is practically unpredictable. Or else they would like to read them out of the congregation of factors. But the sad thing is, the emerging concepts may become deacons, or shamans, or charismatic leaders of that congregation. What then? We can only say then that the social actor, member of a group and part of a fabric of action, is also a potential innovator, whose innovation cannot be perfectly predicted from a knowledge of the group. The social system is not completely closed. Furthermore, the socially problematic character of innovation—will it sell or will it not?—means that those concerned with innovation have

grounds for the hortatory theory. It is possible to *make* the prophecy come true. The major caution is this: what is imaginable differs from what is possible; what is possible differs from what is probable. What is probable can best be determined by the knowledge of context in time and social space—i.e., behavioral social science.

Beyond this problem is that of the relative value of ends. What is worth doing and what is not? More realistically, what are the relative values of ends given the cost of means? Following the thought of Max Weber, we can differentiate between the *zweckrationale* and the *wertrationale*: the former refers to the rationality of given acts for given ends, the latter to the value of given ends in a given way of life. The difficult problem is the latter: How do we determine what is worth doing?

But these are really two sets of problems. Not only do we ask: What is worth doing? but also: What price is worth paying for this thing I want to do? The social scientist as behaviorist can only tell you *what it will cost.* (But this is more than anyone else can tell you with any degree of logical coercion.) If you turn to contemporary, large-scale society, you will find that the true nature of man, the proper conduct of man, is not given. Indeed, alternatives emerge and choice is fought out in bloody combat—and here is the clue. To determine what the self-fufilling prophecy is worth in the language of sacrifice, one is driven to the individual solution: after Luther, Max Weber says, "I do this because I can do no other." We struggle through social combat to determine the nature of what we are. If we are lucky, individually we express our most valued self; collectively we discover and reinforce a valuable character for our society. The problematic nature of the *wertrationale* is the inescapable reason for politics.

THE THIRD CULTURE

C. P. Snow makes two serious errors in his critique of our contemporary intellectual establishments. First, he confuses science, the developing map of the world based on ineluctables and proved by test, with the world of technology—the applied arts. But these arts are in no sense ineluctables; they are matters of choice. Second, he fails to understand the uselessness of physical science for the problems that the humanists underscore. Thus he speaks of problems in economic development and population control, yet these are not products of ignorance in the technologies derived from physical science. They come from cultural and organizational constraints, political weakness, and the lack of applied social science.

In short, the important intellectual force developing today is one that stands *between* the physical sciences and the humanities. Sharing the subject of the latter, the method of the former, the social sciences can show the physicist where he fits in the nature of *social* things: they can also show the humanist *why* the liberal arts are crucial (and perhaps, in the process, dissuade him from his pseudo-scientific drudgeries). Of course the humanist and the physicist, being equally ignorant, will complain that the social sciences are not real sciences like, for example, physics. The answer to that is simple: real or not, social science is the major creator of social fact today. The social fact thus created determines policy which shapes destiny. It was not nuclear physicists who judged the beginning of the cold war—it was men skilled in Russian history, political science, diplomacy. The judgment was one for which physics and Pushkin were rather irrelevant, though Pushkin less so than physics. And to put the shoe on the other foot, the current revolution in Soviet psychology was not brought about by another Pavlov, but by the discovery that Pavlov is inadequate. Learning theory and the study of cognitive processes (largely capitalist innovations) were much more to the point. Dogmas can be afforded only so long; costs mount.

The major danger today is that the social sciences will be subject to premature closure. Policy needs can freeze systems of knowledge long before their results are valid in universal terms; continuity and agreement are required for policy decisions. Yet social science can be a useful tool for increasing our self-knowledge (and therefore our freedom) *only* as long as it remains open-ended and self-correcting. The contingency of knowledge is a difficult thing to remember, yet we forget it at our peril. Perhaps between the chauvinism of a C. P. Snow and the crocodile tears of the humanist who sees history as a projective test lies a valid perspective. Perhaps the social sciences can remain humble before the contingencies of discovery, the ubiquity of error, and the fallibility of judgment, yet stubborn before the problems of understanding human society and its history.

ETHICS, ESTHETICS, AND SOCIAL SCIENCE

It is a strange and exotic view to which we are led by the argument of this essay. Man's belief in what is rests upon a metaphor concerning himself and his world; empirical reality is closely linked with both ethics and esthetics. For the metaphor is implicit in the esthetic component of our experience, in our basic conception, and in our constructed theories or models, while the ethical imperative derives from the view of empirical reality and an image of a hypothetical world, a "model man." Interdependence among the three realms is tangible, as the poets have known for a long time.

Yet it is useful to separate these aspects of our experience. For one thing, keeping in mind the criteria for the social science we will allow into our canon, we are better able to appreciate the nature and value of social science. Its value lies in the fact that it is neither a matter of ethical imperative nor a matter of personal taste. ("Limitation is the source of value.") We must leave it to be just what it is.

To do so we view it as one abstraction among many. It is, however, a systematic abstraction and we have reviewed some of the aspects of its system. It has an order of its own, which may be appreciated in itself, an accomplishment of the human mind. It may also be valued as a tool for working in the

world, a way to help autistic children, poor nations, or states-
men in their tasks. But perhaps most important, it is a way
of improving our philosophy. By editing our beliefs about
what is we implicitly change our notions of what should be;
we escape the toils of various demons and deities created by
our own metaphors. By editing our beliefs we also change our
notions about what is beautiful; we have extended our range
to the artifacts of Africa and Oceania, and we may well find
aspects of African and Oceanic social life equally impressive
once we have recovered from the shock of the new. Utopias
frequently result from simply expanding the range of empirical knowledge.

By insisting that social science is neither a matter of taste,
about which there is no disputing, nor a matter of faith,
which is beyond discourse, we improve our criteria for these
other major realms of experience. Ethics is pre-eminently a
matter of social action and a true appreciation of the limits
of social science has major implications for our ethics. It helps
us to avoid the crude positivism, popular with Marxists and
capitalists alike, which holds that science knows best. Such
vulgarization of social science can only destroy our capacity for
that civic discourse postulated in both the utopias of the past
and the ideologies of the present. Given the ineluctable fact
that human goals are, finally, matters of choice, a proper
knowledge of social science makes clear the limits of choice.

It can also help us with the nature of that choice. Though
social science is a study of limited aspects of our human situation, those aspects are *there*, and they determine much that
concerns us. The belief that aspiration determines all, stated
earlier in the quotation from Johnston's play ("I will take
this world between my two fists and batter it into the symbol
of my heart's desire"), is a major enemy of promise. It leads
to an arrogance toward the tough and splendid nature of the
true facts, or a solipsistic disregard of them, which reflects
neither wisdom nor idealism.

Our approach to the third member of the ancient triad is
also influenced by an acceptance of the true status of social
science. Seeing its power and its limits, we can avoid the

naïveté that blinds us to the beauty inherent in the fine structures of the world and the harsh structures created by men to interpret them. In short, we do not have to make the intellectual sacrifice—the sacrifice of significance.

But we also avoid the naïveté that sees in a vivid description the "full rich concreteness of human life." We do not confuse esthetic standards with the rigorous demands of science. Sloppy reporting without concern for validity or reliability is not allowed to masquerade as fact; it is seen more accurately as the raw material of fact. Knowing what social science is *not* allows us to pay due homage to the great engines of human sensibility and metaphorical thought without abusing them by asking them to perform tasks beyond their capacities.

In the end, we all create our own *bricolage*. Nobody lives by science but nobody lives without it and the same holds for our esthetics and our ethics. We are all finally forced to complete our thought in our actions; but those actions are never complete. This completion of thought in action corresponds to Lévi-Strauss' interpretation of "dialectical reason":

> In my view dialectical reason is always constitutive: it is the bridge, forever extended and improved, which analytical reason throws out over an abyss; it is unable to see the further shore but it knows that it is there, even should it be constantly receding. The term dialectical reason thus covers the perpetual efforts analytical reason must make to reform itself if it aspires to account for language, society, and thought . . .

Science is a formal creation in the face of nature, one that aims to tame nature through prediction and control congruent with a larger order than science itself. Ethics reflects a commitment, a faith; all human societies believe their own formulation to be correct.

Underlying both ethics and science may be, simply, esthetics. Looking at the range of human moral systems, *weltanschauungen,* one is impressed with their intrinsically dramatistic quality. The good man seeks escape from the wheel of transmigration, he struggles for righteousness, he emulates mythical heroes, he makes the great sacrifice, tames the wild spirit. Why, we may ask, these particular metaphors? Why this given direction for a life or a society? Why this way of organizing desire? The answer may be: Thus we created it.

What we have created we can recreate, indefinitely.

NOTES and REFERENCES

[1]

5 Karl Mannheim's sociology of knowledge is developed in *Ideology and Utopia* (Harcourt, Brace, 1936).

5 For a representative statement of the Marxist argument, see "Excerpts from 'A Contribution to the Critique of Political Economy,'" in *Marx and Engels: Basic Writings on Politics and Philosophy*, Lewis S. Feuer, ed. (Anchor, 1953). Included in this article is Marx's famous statement that: "It is not the consciousness of men that determines their existence, but, on the contrary, their social existence that determines their consciousness" (p. 43).

5 The notion of marginality emerges in Georg Simmel, "The Web of Group Affiliations," in *Conflict and The Web of Group Affiliations*, Reinhard Bendix, trans. (Free Press, 1955).

7 The procedural norms of scientific inquiry are discussed at length by Alfred Schutz in "The World of Scientific Inquiry" in *Collected Papers: The Problem of Social Reality* Maurice Natanson, ed. (The Hague: Martinus Nijhoff, 1962), especially pp. 245-259.

7 Comparisons of Negro and white intelligence, including the army test results, are summarized in Robert D. North, "The Intelligence of American Negroes," *Research Reports*, 3 (1955), 2-8.

7 For a particularly fine study refuting race differences see Otto Klineberg, "The Influence of the Northern Environment of the Intelligence Scores of Negroes," in *The Language of Social Research*, Paul F. Lazarsfeld and Morris Rosenberg, eds. (Free Press, 1955), pp. 175-183.

13 M. Sherif describes his famous experiment in "Group Influences Upon the Formation of Norms and Atti-

tudes" in *Readings in Social Psychology*, T. M. New-
comb and E. L. Hartley, eds. (Holt, 1947).

14 For an analysis of the Metropolitan St. Louis Survey,
see Scott Greer, "Dilemmas of Action Research on the
Metropolitan Problem" in *Community Political Systems*, Morris Janowitz, ed. (Free Press, 1961).

15 Classic statements of the "mass society" theory include
José Ortega y Gasset, *The Revolt of the Masses* (Nor-
ton, 1932); Oswald Spengler, *Decline of the West*,
Charles Francis Atkinson, trans. (Knopf, 1926); Emile
Durkheim, *The Division of Labor in Society*, George
Simpson, trans. (Free Press, 1949); Ferdinand Tönnies,
*Gemeinschaft and Gesellschaft (Community and So-
ciety)* Charles P. Loomis, trans. (Michigan State Uni-
versity Press, 1957).

15 Social area analysis as an approach to the study of
urban differentiation was developed in Eshref Shevky
and Marilyn Williams, *The Social Areas of Los Angeles*
(University of California Press, 1949); and Eshref
Shevky and Wendell Bell, *Social Area Analysis* (Stanford University Press, 1955).

16 For Wirth's original statement, see Louis Wirth, "Urbanism as a Way of Life," *American Journal of Sociology*, 44 (1938).

16 Some of the research stimulated by the findings of the
Metropolitan St. Louis Survey is discussed in *The New
Urbanization* Scott Greer *et. al*, eds. (St. Martin's Press,
1968).

17 In *The Polish Peasant in Europe and America* (University of Chicago Press, 1918), W. I. Thomas and
Florian Znaniecki pioneered the study of ethnic differentiation and social organization.

17 Robert Merton discusses policy needs and philosophy
as alternative methods for defining the problems of
social inquiry in *Social Theory and Social Structure*
(Free Press, 1957), pp. 207–224.

[II]

24 Emile Durkheim argues that social science is properly
the study of "social fact" in *The Rules of Sociological
Method*, Sarah A. Solovay and John H. Mueller, trans.
(University of Chicago Press, 1938, first published 1895).
His classic application of this method to the study of
human behavior is *Suicide*, John A. Spaulding and
George Simpson, trans. (Free Press, 1951, first published
1897).

[III]

29 John James presented his discussion of "the neutrality
of the human nervous system" in lectures to his students at the University of California at Los Angeles,
1949.

29 Marshall McLuhan comments on the changing nature
of human sensibilities in *Understanding Media: the
Extensions of Man* (McGraw Hill, 1964).

29 Susanne K. Langer writes of the ability of symbols to
structure the apprehensions of man, in *Philosophy in
a New Key* (New American Library, 1942) , p. 29.

32 John Dewey emphasized the importance of one's prior
frame of reference in the determination of perception
in *Logic: The Theory of Inquiry* (Holt, 1938), especially p. 228. The social origins of this frame itself were
noted by Charles Horton Cooley in an early formulation, *Social Organization* (Scribner's, 1909).

33 An analysis of phrenology as a scientific enterprise appears in John D. Davies, *Phrenology, Fad, and Science*
(Yale University Press, 1955). The Lombrosian method
for identifying "criminal types" is presented in Cesare
Lombroso, *Crime, Its Causes and Remedies*, H. P.
Horton, trans. (Little, Brown, 1911), and in Gina Lombroso Ferrero, *Criminal Man According to the classification of Cesare Lombroso* (Putman, 1911). Factual
studies using the Lombrosian method are reported in
Alfred Lindesmith and Yale Levin, "The Lombrosian
Myth in Criminology" *American Journal of Sociology,*
42 (March 1937), 653–671; and in Yale Levin and
Alfred Lindesmith, "English Ecology and Criminology
of the Past Century, " *Journal of Criminal Law and
Criminology,* 27 (March–April, 1957), 801–816. Both
phrenology and the Lombrosian method are discussed
in George B. Vold, "Physical Type Theories," *Theoretical Criminology* (Oxford University Press, 1958),
pp. 43–74; and in Arthur E. Fink, *The Causes of
Crime: Biological Theories in the United States,
1800–1915,* (University of Pennsylvania Press, 1938).

34 Clyde Kluckhohn reports that the Eskimo language
includes thirty words for our word "snow" in "Culture and Behavior," *Handbook of Social Psychology,*
Vol. II, Gardner Lindzey, ed. (Addison-Wesley, 1954),
pp. 937–938.

34 For a brilliant insight into the intellectual orientations
which do and do not produce a scientific frame of
reference, see Claude Lévi-Strauss, *The Savage Mind*

(University of Chicago Press, 1966), especially Chapter
9, "History and Dialectic."

35 Evidence discrediting the interest of early criminology
in mental traits is summarized by Karl F. Schuessler
and D. R. Cressey, in "Personality Characteristics of
Criminals," *American Journal of Sociology,* 55 (March
1950), 476–484.

35 The famous Sutherland theory appears in the Edwin
H. Sutherland and Donald R. Cressey text, *The Principles of Criminology* (Lippincott, 1960), Chapter IV,
especially pp. 77–79.

36 Representative of the studies that used and expanded
the Sutherland theory by their attention to subculture
are those reported in *The Other Side: Perspectives on
Deviance,* Howard S. Becker, ed. (Free Press, 1964).

[IV]

37 Susanne Langer discusses the evolutionary school of
symbolization at some length with specific reference
to the works of its major exponents, *Philosophy in a
New Key* (New American Library, 1942), pp. 33–39.

37 That the assumptions of this school, with their Pavlovian implications, were operative in postrevolutionary
Russian education is apparent in Neil O'Connor's discussion of "Soviet Educational Psychology," in *Communist Education,* Edmund J. King, ed. (Bobbs-Merrill, 1963), pp. 38–49.

38 The experiment with deaf-mutes from which we can
infer the importance of symbolization to human
thought is cited by David Crech and Richard S.
Crutchfield in *Elements of Psychology* (Knopf, 1958) ,
p. 474.

38–39 For George Herbert Mead's elaboration of this idea,
see *Mind, Self and Society,* C. W. Morris, ed. (University of Chicago Press, 1934); for the metaphor of the
game, see specifically pp. 149–164.

39 Other scholars whose studies of the relationship between symbolization and human thought deserve mention are Charles Horton Cooley, whose pioneer study
of "The Early Use of Self-Words by a Child" appeared
in *Psychological Review* 15 (1908), 339–357, and Jean
Piaget, whose book *The Language and Thought of the
Child* (Harcourt, Brace, 1926) expanded the notions of
Cooley and Mead. A useful summary of the ideas in
this book is included in John H. Flavell's *The Develop-
mental Psychology of Jean Piaget* (Van Nostrand,
1963), pp. 270–275.

39 Langer's challenge to these ideas is presented in her chapter on "Symbolic Transformation," especially pp. 39-54, in *Philosophy in a New Key*.

40 See Langer, pp. 43-45.

41 See Langer, p. 47.

41 The functions of ritual in maintaining group solidarity are proposed by Emile Durkheim in *The Elementary Forms of Religious Life*, Joseph Swain, trans. (Free Press, 1954, first published 1912).

42 For a recent work on sleep, including the relationship between symbolization and dreams, see Gay Gaer Luce and Julius Segal, *Sleep* (Coward-McCann, 1966).

43 See Langer, p. 70.

44 Paul Bohannon analyzes the judicial behavior of the Tiv in *Justice and Judgement Among the Tiv* (Oxford University Press, 1957). An excellent review of this book by Victor Ayoub is available in *Community Political Systems*, Morris Janowitz, ed. (Free Press, 1961), pp. 237-250.

45 For a fuller discussion of signification, denotation, and connotation, see Langer's chapter on "The Logic of Signs and Symbols," in *Philosophy in a New Key*, especially pp. 54-74.

47 Silent barter among primitive tribes is described by E. Adamson Hoebel, *Man in the Primitive World* (McGraw-Hill, 1949), p. 350.

[v]

49 See Paul Radin's example of "primitive pragmatism" in *Primitive Man as Philosopher* (Dover, 1957, first published 1927), pp. 15-16.

51 Max Weber proclaimed the scientific "disenchantment of the world" in his now famous article "Science As a Vocation," in *From Max Weber*, H. H. Gerth and C. Wright Mills, trans. and eds. (Oxford University Press, 1958).

51 Susanne K. Langer notes the place of history in this disenchantment in *Philosophy in a New Key* (New American Library, 1942), p. 233.

52 Max Gluckman tells the story of the Nuer father in a fine article on the work of Evans—Pritchard, "The Logic of African Science and Witchcraft," in *Readings in Anthropology*, E. Adamson Hoebel et al., eds. McGraw Hill, 1955), p. 273.

53-54 Studies of resistance to technological change at various occupational levels include: Lester Coch and John R. P. French, Jr., "Overcoming Resistance to Change,"

Human Relations I (1948), 512–532; Melville Dalton, "Conflicts Between Staff and Line Managerial Officers," *American Sociological Review* (June 1950), 342–351; Ida R. Hoos, "When the Computer Takes Over the Office," *Harvard Business Review* (July–August 1960), 102–112; B. B. Gardner and David F. Moore, *Human Relations in Industry: Organizational and Administrative Behavior* (Richard D. Irwin, 1964), pp. 455–462.

54–55 A useful discussion of the method whereby the social scientist infers meaning through borrowed frames of reference is Howard S. Becker's "Problems of Inference and Proof in Participant Observation," *American Sociological Review*, 23 (December 1958), 652–660.

55 An account of the Eskimo's treatment of an infirm mother can be found in E. Adamson Hoebel, *Man in the Primitive World* (McGraw Hill, 1949), p. 295.

55 For a brilliant fictional treatment of the problems involved in transplanting bureaucratic systems into non-Western societies, see Anthony Burgess, *The Long Day Wanes: A Malayan Trilogy* (Norton, 1964).

55 Intra-societal differences in frames of reference are examined by Leonard Schatzman and Anselm Strauss, "Social Class and Modes of Communication," *American Journal of Sociology*, 60 (1954–55), 329–338; and by Herbert Gans, *The Urban Villagers: Group and Class In the Life of Italian-Americans* (Free Press, 1962).

58 That the preconceptions of social scientists may influence the nature of their findings has been dramatically illustrated in community-power research. For one report, see Claire Gilbert, "The Study of Community Power: A Summary and a Test" in *The New Urbanization*, Scott Greer, et al., eds. (St. Martin's Press, 1968).

58 Phenomenology was introduced to American sociology by Alfred Schutz, *Collected Papers: The Problem of Social Reality*, Maurice Natanson, ed. (The Hague: Martinus Nijhoff, 1962). For a sample of current research deriving from Schutz's formulations, see Harold Garfinkel, *Studies in Ethnomethodology*, (Prentice Hall, 1967), and the reviews of this book in "Review Symposium," *American Sociological Review*, 33 (1968), 122–130.

[VI]

63 This chapter leans heavily on Alfred North Whitehead, *Science and the Modern World* (New American Library, 1925).

63 Whitehead, pp. 47–48.
63–64 Norman Campbell, *What Is Science?* (Dover, 1952, first published 1921), p. 72.
64 For a more complete discussion of "practical vision," see Susanne K. Langer, *Philosophy in a New Key* (New American Library, 1942), Chapter X.
64 The development of a faith in universal order which made possible scientific vision is traced by Whitehead in the first chapter of *Science and the Modern World*.
64 The early Greek foundations for this emerging faith are described by H. D. F. Kitto in *The Greeks* (Aldine, 1964, first published 1951), Chapter 5, "The Polis."
66 John Herman Randall, *The Making of the Modern Mind* (Houghton-Mifflin, 1954), p. 36.
67 Whitehead, p. 19.
67 Randall discusses the spirit of Newtonian science in a chapter entitled "The Newtonian World-Machine," in *The Making of the Modern Mind*.
68 "Rickover phenomenon" refers to a discovery of one of my students, who observed that a famous submarine admiral was given a fictitious expertise in the psychology and social organization of education. *Gloria mundo.*
68 Whitehead, *Science and the Modern World*, pp. 23, 42.
69 In discussing the scientific frame, Whitehead suggests two precautions that help one avoid "tunnel vision," *Science and the Modern World*, p. 24.
69 Whitehead, *Science and the Modern World*, p. 45.
69 Whitehead, *Science and the Modern World*, p. 46.
70 The imaginative component in inductive logic is illustrated with the Galilean example in F. S. C. Northorp, *The Logic of the Sciences and the Humanities* (Macmillan, 1947), Chapter 1.
71 Whitehead, *Science and the Modern World*, p. 74–75.
71 Whitehead, *Science and the Modern World*, p. 76.
72 The poem is Blake's "Mock on, Mock on, Voltaire, Rousseau."

[VII]

73 This chapter obviously owes a great deal to Alfred North Whitehead's *Science and the Modern World* (New American Library, 1925), Chapter 10, "Abstraction," pp. 142–155.
75–76 Whitehead, *Science and the Modern World*, pp. 147–148.
76 Whitehead, *Science and the Modern World*, p. 53.
77 For Whitehead's discussion of the components of an

abstractive hierarchy" see Whitehead, *Science and the Modern World*, p. 151 ff.

78 "Analysis" and "Synthesis" are discussed by Whitehead, *Science and the Modern World*, p. 147 ff.

79 Whitehead, *Science and the Modern World*, p. 143.

80–81 For insight into groups as abstractions representing interdependent parts, see Nicholas J. Spykman, *The Social Theory of Georg Simmel* (University of Chicago Press, 1925), Chapter I, "The Concept of Society as Form and as Content," pp. 26–34: "A social group consists, in the last analysis, in mental attitudes or psychological occurrences within the minds of individuals; but the fact that these attitudes and occurrences are the product of mutual determinations and reciprocal influences creates a dynamic functional relationship between the individuals, and that dynamic functional relationship creates and is the unity of the group. The group is a unity because of this process or these processes of reciprocal influencing between the individuals. The state is a unity because between its citizens there is a more intimate exchange of reciprocal influences than between these citizens and those of other states" (p. 27).

See also Georg Simmel, "Persistence of Social Groups," *American Journal of Sociology* 3 (1897–98), 662–698; Georg Simmel, "The Problem of Sociology," *Publications of the American Academy of Political and Social Science*, 161 (December 3, 1895), 412–422; and Georg Simmel, *The Sociology of Georg Simmel*, Kurt H. Wolff, trans. and ed. (Free Press, 1950). Thus: "Sociology asks what happens to men and by what rules they behave, not insofar as they unfold their understandable individual existences in their totalities, but insofar as they form groups and are determined by their group existence because of interaction. . . . The topics of its researches certainly arise in a process of abstraction . . . from concrete reality, performed under the guidance of the concept society" (pp. 11–12).

82 Whitehead, *Science and the Modern World*, p. 175–176.

[VIII]

83 For a sample of the anthropological linguistics of Benjamin Lee Whorf, see *Language, Thought, and Reality*, John B. Carroll, ed. (Massachusetts Institute of Technology Press, 1957).

85 In *The Poverty of Historicism* (Harper, 1957), Karl R. Popper analyzes the assumptions of historical determinism and the shortcomings of its propositions when used as empirical theory.

87 Freud's Oedipal complex theory of father-son relations is refuted by Bronislaw Malinowski in *Sex and Repression in Savage Society* (Harcourt, Brace, 1927).

87 One of the best summaries of the instinct theories of human behavior is L. L. Bernard's *An Introduction to Sociology: A Naturalistic Account of Man's Adjustment to his World* (Crowell, 1942), Chapter XXII.

89 Classic studies documenting the tendency for goal-oriented groups to become ends in themselves are Edward A. Shils and Morris Janowitz, "Cohesion and Disintegration in the Wehrmacht in World War II," *Public Opinion Quarterly*, 12 (Summer 1948), 280–315; F. J. Roethlisberger and W. J. Dickson, *Management and the Worker* (Harvard University Press, 1939), Part IV; Samuel A. Stouffer et. al., *The American Soldier* (Princeton University Press, 1949).

90 Susanne Langer discusses the forms of expression that are and are not amenable to logical argument in her chapter on "Discursive and Presentational Forms" in *Philosophy in a New Key* (New American Library, 1942), p. 81.

91 Langer, p. 82.

93 Studies of "stress in the role of the foreman" include Donald E. Wray, "Marginal Men of Industry: The Foreman" *American Journal of Sociology*, 54 (1948–49), 298–301; and Burleigh B. Gardner and William Foote Whyte, "The Man in the Middle: Position and Problems of the Foreman," *Applied Anthropology* (1945), 1–28.

[IX]

96 Melville Herskovitz describes the Dahomean census in *Dahomey: An Ancient West African Kingdom* (J. J. Augustin, 1938), Vol. 1; pp. 113–114; Vol. 2, pp. 72–79.

96 Mathematics as a system of abstract logic proceeding from a set of postulates is discussed by Alfred North Whitehead in *Science and the Modern World* (New American Library, 1925), p. 31 (italics mine).

97 Whitehead, *Science and the Modern World*, p. 29.

98 Whitehead, *Science and the Modern World*, p. 30.

98 See Robert F. Winch, The Modern Family (Holt, Rinehart, & Winston, 1964), for a useful summary of

current thought in the sociology of the family.

99 Arthur Bentley proposes five kinds of space in *Inquiry Into Inquiries: Essays in Social Theory*, Sidney Ratner, ed. (Beacon, 1954), p. 62.

100 The space–time ratio is a means of examining social space is discussed by Scott Greer in *The Emerging City: Myth and Reality* (Free Press, 1962), pp. 78–79; and in *Governing the Metropolis* (Wiley, 1962), pp. 9–15.

100 John Friedman's ideas about "interactional space" were brought to my attention in conversation with him.

100 Bentley turns to the problem of social *dimensions* in *Inquiry Into Inquiries*, pp. 94–95.

100 Paul F. Lazarsfeld and A. H. Barton address the problem of social dimensions in their discussion of "attribute space." See "Qualitative Measurement in the Social Sciences: Classification, Typologies, and Indices" in *The Policy Sciences* D. Lerner and H. D. Lasswell, eds. (Stanford University Press, 1951), especially pp. 155–192.

101 For the Shevky approach to urban analysis, see Eshref Shevky and Marilyn Williams, *The Social Areas of Los Angeles* (University of California Press, 1949); and Eshref Shevky and Wendell Bell, *Social Area Analysis* (Stanford University Press, 1955).

[x]

109 Alfred North Whitehead traces the development of Western man's faith in natural order in the first chapter of *Science and the Modern World* (New American Library, 1925), "The Origins of Modern Science," 9–25.

109 That scientific investigation requires intersubjective verification of observations is emphasized by Norman Campbell in *What Is Science?* (Dover, 1952, first published 1921), p. 27 (italics mine).

109 Intersubjective verification, taken alone, however, does not assure accurate conclusions—as illustrated by the agreement which can be obtained in the case of mirages. The example in the text comes from James H. Gordon, "Mirages," *Annual Report of the Board of Regents of the Smithsonian Institution*, Publication 4392 (1959) pp. 327–346.

112–113 Kingsley Davis' studies of the effects of isolation on child development should alert us to the difficulties encountered in attempting to define "social" as a unit for inquiry in terms of "human" behavior. See "Extreme Social Isolation of A Child," *American Journal of Sociology* 45 (January 1940), 554–564; and "Final Note on a Case of Extreme Isolation," *American Journal of Sociology* 50 (March 1947), 432–437.

114 In a little-read sequel to "Urbanism as a Way of Life," Louis Wirth questioned the usefulness of the rural-urban distinctions he had described in the earlier article. He had come to feel that the meanings of these terms were obscured by the variations within the categories and by their overall similarity. For this later statement, see "Rural–Urban Differences" in *Community Life and Social Policy: Selected Papers by Louis Wirth*, Elizabeth Marvick and Albert J. Reiss, Jr., eds. (University of Chicago Press, 1956), pp. 172–176.

115 Edwin Lemert questioned the usefulness of the folk definitions of crimes and criminals in *Social Pathology* (McGraw-Hill, 1950).

117 Campbell, p. 71.

118 For a fuller discussion of "deviant case analysis," see Part C in *The Language of Social Research*, Paul F. Lazarsfeld and Morris Rosenberg, eds. (Free Press, 1965).

118 Donald Cressey's *Other People's Money: A Study in the Social Psychology of Embezzlement* (Free Press, 1953) is an example of skillful use of this approach to theory building.

120 The case for the causality concept in social research has been stated by such men as Robert MacIver, *Social Causation* (Ginn, 1942); and George Lundberg, *Foundations of Sociology* (Macmillan, 1939) and *Can Science Save Us?* (Longmans, Green, 1947).

122 See Samuel A. Stouffer, "Intervening Opportunities: A Theory Relating to Mobility and Distance," *American Sociological Review* V (1940), 845–867, for a report on the type of "law" Stouffer was able to establish for the prediction of migration distances.

122 Emile Durkheim, *Suicide,* John A. Spaulding and George Simpson, trans. (Free Press, 1951, first published 1897).

124 Given Durkheim's original formulation, Robert Merton could attempt a more precise specification of concepts, in an article originally published as "Social Structure and Anomie," *American Journal of Sociology* (1938), 672–682.

124 Campbell, p. 97.

[XI]

126 The discussion of mathematics presented in this chapter draws much from Norman Campbell, *What Is Science?* (Dover, 1952, first published 1921), chapter 6; and Alfred North Whitehead, *Science and the Modern World* (New American Library, 1925), Chapter 2.

127 Campbell, p. 11.

128 Campbell, p. 122.

129 The notion of "felicific calculus" was developed by Jeremy Bentham, *The Works of Jeremy Bentham*.

129 Difficulties arise in applying real number to social science data when variables are not continuous, as with the Harold L. Wilensky finding reported in "Mass Society and Mass Culture: Interdependence or Independence?" *American Sociological Review*, 29 (April 1964), 173–197.

130 Similarly, the usefulness of real number is limited when such factors as race are able to influence the value of numerically measurable dollars. See Beverly Duncan and Philip M. Hauser, *Housing a Metropolis —Chicago* (Free Press, 1960).

130 Several useful summaries of the major voting studies are available, including: S. M. Lipset, P. F. Barton, and A. H. Linz, "The Psychology of Voting: An Analysis of Political Behavior," in *Handbook of Social Psychology*, Vol. II, Gardner Lindzey, ed. (Addison–Wesley, 1954), pp. 1124–1176; S. J. Eldersveld, "Theory and Method in Voting Behavior Research," in *Political Behavior: A Reader in Theory and Research* Heinz Eulau, S. J. Eldersfeld, and Morris Janowitz, eds. (Free Press, 1956), pp. 267–274; E. Burdick and A. J. Brodbeck, eds. *American Voting Behavior* (Free Press, 1959).

131 Paul F. Lazarsfeld, Bernard Berelson, and Hazel Gaudet, *The People's Choice* (Columbia University Press, 1948); Bernard Berelson, Paul F. Lazarsfeld, and William N. McPhee, *Voting: A Study of Opinion Formation in a Presidential Campaign* (University of Chicago Press, 1954).

131 Ernest S. Bogardus, "Racial Distance in the United States During the Past Thirty Years," *Sociology and Social Research* 43 (1958), 127–135; and *Social Distance* (Antioch, 1959).

132 Campbell, p. 133.

133 Whitehead, *Science and the Modern World*, pp. 33–34.

134–35 Peter M. Blau, *Dynamics of Bureaucracy* (University of Chicago Press, 1955); Peter M. Blau, *Bureaucracy in Modern Society* (Random House, 1956); Robert K. Merton, A. P. Gray, B. Hockey, and H. C. Selvin, eds. *Reader in Bureaucracy* (Free Press, 1952); Peter Blau and W. R. Scott, *Formal Organizations* (Chandler, 1962).

135 Fred Cottrell, *Technological Change and the Future of Railroads* (Northwestern University Transportation Center, 1962).

[XII]

138 P. M. Worsley describes the logic and character of the postwar cargo cults in "Millenarian Movements in Melanesia," *Rhodes-Livingston Institute Journal* (1957), 18–31. Reprinted by Bobbs-Merrill, "A–248," *Reprint Series in Anthropology*.

140 For Robert Merton's discussion of "middle range theory" see *Social Theory and Social Structure* (Free Press, 1957), pp. 5–10.

140 Hans Zetterberg attempted to axiomatize Durkheim in "On Axiomatic Theories in Sociology," in *The Language of Social Research* Paul F. Lazarsfeld and Morris Rosenberg, eds. (Free Press, 1955), pp. 533–540.

140 An up-to-date report on current research into the use of mathematical models is James S. Coleman, "Mathematical Models and Computer Simulation" in *Handbook of Modern Sociology*, Robert L. Faris, ed. (Rand-McNally, 1964), pp. 1027–1062. For further discussion of the various ways in which models are used see May Brodbeck, "Models, Meanings and Theories," and Herbert Hochberg, "Axiomatic Systems, Formalization and Scientific Theories" in *Symposium of Sociological Theory*, Llewellyn Gross, ed. (Row, Peterson, 1959).

143 The use in voting research of notions like social attitude or tendencies to act expresses a transfer of the meteorological metaphor to social science. Reviews of the major studies in this area were cited in the notes to Chapter 11. Louis Leon Thurstone called such tendencies to act *Vectors of Mind* (University of Chicago Press, 1953).

144 Gunnar Myrdal carried the metaphor a step further when he proposed to examine a situation resulting from a conflict between attitudes in a society, *An American Dilemma* (Harper, 1944).

144 The interest of social scientists in the metaphor of the game was signaled by George Herbert Mead, *Mind,*

Self, and Society, C. W. Morris, ed. (University of Chicago Press, 1934), pp. 149–164.

146 See Scott Greer, *Social Organization* (Random House, 1955) for an examination of extended family relations in the Trobriand Islands, and Melville Dalton, "Conflicts Between Staff and Line Managerial Officers," *American Sociological Review* (June, 1950), 342–351.

147 Donald Campbell's pithy description of the evolutionary process appears in "Variation and Selective Retention in Socio-Cultural Evolution," in *Social Change in the Developing Areas: A Reinterpretation of Evolutionary Theory*, Herbert R. Barringer, George I. Blanksten, and Raymond W. Mack, eds. (Schenkman, 1965), pp. 19–49.

147 See Emile Durkheim, *The Division of Labor in Society*, George Simpson, trans. (Free Press, 1947, first published 1893) for his famous application of the organic metaphor to the study of societal evolution.

[XIII]

150 The "pie-cut" approach to the etiology of deviation was discussed with me by the criminologist Donald R. Cressey, a veteran of many "commissions."

153 For a concrete example of the problems of analyzing complex social systems, and one primitive answer, see Scott Greer, *Last Man In, Racial Access to Union Power* (Free Press, 1959).

154 The use of "nonresponsive measures" in the study of organizational overlap in groups of carpenters is reported in James W. Moorhead, "A Theory of Intergroup Relations, A Study of Carpenters' Unions and Construction Companies" Unpublished M. A. Thesis, Northwestern University, 1960).

157 A major eclectic, Gaetano Mosca is known to social scientists in the United States chiefly through *The Ruling Class* (McGraw-Hill, 1939).

158 For the work of the most ambitious contemporary "grand theory," see Talcott Parsons, *The Social System* (Free Press, 1951) and *Societies: An Evolutionary and Comparative Perspective*, (Prentice-Hall, 1966).

[XIV]

160 The succinct statement of Bentley's philosophy of inquiry is expanded in *Inquiry into Inquiries: Essays in Social Theory*, Sidney Ratner, ed. (Beacon Press, 1954), pp. 307–312.

161 The major and too little known study of social attitudes as predicters of action is reported in R. T. LaPiere, "The Sociological Significance of Measurable Attitudes," *American Sociological Review* 3 (1938), 175–182.

161 For the best presentation of the operationalism of the 1930's see George Lundberg, *Foundations of Sociology* (Macmillan, 1939).

161–162 Percy W. Bridgman's major statement is contained in *The Logic of Modern Physics* (Macmillan, 1928). His second thoughts are presented in Percy W. Bridgman, *Reflections of a Physicist,* 2nd ed. (Philosophical Library, 1955).

161–162 Bentley's comments are found in *Inquiry into Inquiries,* pp. 119–120.

162–163 Chapin's efforts at operationalizing social status are found in F. S. Chapin, *Contemporary American Institutions* (Harper, 1935), Chapter XIX, "A Measurement of Social Status," especially "1931 Scale for Rating Living Room Equipment," pp. 383–386.

163 For Redfield's use of cross-sectional data in the analysis of social development, see Robert Redfield's *The Folk Culture of the Yucatan* (University of Chicago Press, 1941). For a later statement see *The Primitive World and its Transformations* (Cornell University Press, 1953).

164 Donald Cressey's method to explain past chains of causation through comparative study of the results is presented in *Other People's Money: A Study in the Social Psychology of Embezzlement* (Free Press, 1953).

164 The "lurking variables" underlying the correlation of Negro population and Republican votes are explicated by V. O. Key in *Southern Politics* (Knopf, 1949).

165 For a sample of Lewin's work with contrived groups see Kurt Lewin and Ronald Lippitt, "An Experimental Approach to the Study of Autocracy and Democracy: A Preliminary Note," *Sociometry,* I, (January–April 1938) and Kurt Lewin, "Experiments in Social Space," reprinted in *Resolving Social Conflicts: Selected Papers on Group Dynamics, 1935–1946,* Gertrud Weiss Lewin, ed. (Harper, 1948).

165 For a synthesis, see M. and Carolyn W. Sherif, *Groups in Harmony and Tension: An Integration of Studies on Intergroup Relations* (Harper, 1953).

166 The distinction between the logic of discovery and the logic of proof is stated well in Hans Reichenbach, *The*

Rise of Scientific Philosophy (University of California Press, 1951).

167 Blumer's notions of sensitizing theory were first stated in his article, "What is Wrong with Social Theory?" *American Sociological Review* 19 (February 1954), 3–10.

168 The three princes of Serendip were introduced to sociologists by Robert K. Merton in *Social Theory and Social Structure* (Free Press, 1957), pp. 103–108.

168 My adventures with indices of participation in union organizations and their meanings are reported in *Last Man In, Racial Access to Union Power* (Free Press, 1959).

169 A similar mistake, uncorrected, is reported in David L. and Mary A. Hatch, "Criteria of Social Status as Derived from Marriage Announcements in the 'New York Times'" *American Sociological Review,* 12 (August 1947), 396–403.

171–172 The series of studies flowing from Lazarsfeld's original work on voting are reported in Paul F. Lazarsfeld, Bernard Berelson, and Hazel Gaudet, *The People's Choice,* 2nd ed. (Columbia University Press, 1948).

172 E. Katz, "The Two-Step Flow of Communication," *Public Opinion Quarterly,* 21 (1957), 61–78; E. Katz and Paul F. Lazarsfeld, *Personal Influence* (Free Press, 1955); B. R. Berelson, P. F. Lazarsfeld, and W. N. McPhee, *Voting* (University of Chicago Press, 1954).

172 Robert K. Merton's work on localities and cosmopolites appears in *Social Theory and Social Structure* (Free Press, 1957), pp. 387–420.

[xv]

181 F. S. C. Northrop's effort to develop an empirical proof for the good is best stated in *The Logic of the Sciences and the Humanities* (Macmillan, 1947), especially Chapter XVII, "The Criterion of the Good State."

182 For a discussion of a society which invented a non-playable game with disastrous consequences, see Jules Henry, *Jungle People* (J. J. Augustin, 1941), pp. 60–63.

183 For an extensive discussion of Levi-Strauss' concept of *bricolage* see *The Savage Mind* (University of Chicago Press, 1966), pp. 16–35.

[xvi]

186 The degree to which we succeed in the simple "finding of facts" in one important area is discussed by Daniel

Bell in *The End of Ideology* (Free Press, 1960), especially Chapter 8, "The Myth of Crime Waves: The Actual Decline of Crime in the United States."

187 Howard S. Becker in *Outsiders* (Free Press, 1951) discusses other "found facts"; see especially Chapter 4, "Marijuana Use and Social Control."

188 For a poignant discussion of "the disenchantment of the world," see Max Weber, "Science as a Vocation," in *From Max Weber*, H. H. Gerth and C. Wright Mills, trans. and eds. (Oxford University Press, 1958).

188 The true nature of poverty and some of its causes in contemporary America are admirably discussed in Harold L. Wilensky and Charles N. Lebeaux, *Industrial Society and Social Welfare* (Free Press, 1965).

189 The quotation concerning British Town Planners is from Lloyd Rodwin, who discusses their perplexities at length in *The British New Towns Policy: Problems and Implications* (Harvard University Press, 1956), p. 187.

189 The ways in which by assuming a "power structure" we may solidify or even create a structure of power are described in Martin Meyerson and Edward C. Banfield, *Politics, Planning and the Public Interest* (Free Press, 1955).

189 The literature on ecology as a metaphor useful in describing cities is immense; the seminal writings include Robert E. Park, Ernest W. Burgess, and Roderick D. McKenzie, *The City* (University of Chicago Press, 1925); Ernest W. Burgess, *Urban Community* (University of Chicago Press, 1925); Robert E. Park, *Human Communities* (Free Press, 1952).

190 For a lively discussion of the 1964 Republican campaign and the folk theory underlying it see Theodore White, *The Making of the President, 1964* (Antheneum, 1965).

191 The strange career of Urban Renewal is recounted in Scott Greer, *Urban Renewal and American Cities: The Dilemma of Democratic Intervention* (Bobbs-Merrill, 1965).

191 The destructive nature of much therapy in mental institutions is detailed by Erving Goffman in *Asylums* (Aldine, 1961).

192 The notion that the metropolitan area is loosely organized, divided, and integrated by "games" is pungently put forth by Norton E. Long in "The Local Community as an Ecology of Games," *American*

Journal of Sociology, LXVI (November 1958), 251–261.

194 Among those who argue that the wage incentive is not necessary is Robert Theobald in *The Guaranteed Income: Next Step in Economic Evolution* (Doubleday, 1966); for the Trobriand Islanders' incentives to work see Bronislaw Malinowski, *Coral Gardens and Their Magic* (Indiana University Press, 1965). I have learned of the Norwegian experience through conversation and the public lectures of my colleague, Bernard Beck, who has carried out extensive observations of welfare practices in Scandinavia.

[XVII]

196 Alfred North Whitehead, *Science and the Modern World* (New American Library, 1925), Chapter 3, "The Century of Genius."

198 For the controversy over the "'two cultures" see C. P. Snow, *The Two Cultures and the Scientific Revolution* (Cambridge University Press, 1959), and the attack by F. R. Leavis, *Two Cultures? The Significance of C. P. Snow, with an Essay on Sir Charles Snow's Rede Lecture* (Pantheon, 1963). It's all wrong-headed but it's a lot of fun.

199 Northrop's insistence on separating the esthetic and the theoretico-deducive aspects of experience and action is discussed from various viewpoints in *The Logic of the Sciences and the Humanities* (Macmillan, 1947).

200 Robert K. Merton, in a well-known article, first coined the phrase "the self-fulfilling prophecy"; see *Social Theory and Social Structure* (Free Press, 1957), pp. 421–436.

201 Max Weber's distinction between *wertrationale* and *zweckrationale* is specified and applied in two famous essays, "Science as a Vocation," and "Politics as a Vocation," in *From Max Weber*, H. H. Gerth and C. Wright Mills, trans. and eds. (Oxford University Press, 1958).

205 The formulation of "dialectical reasoning" is Claude Lévi-Strauss' in *The Savage Mind* (University of Chicago Press, 1966), p. 246.

INDEX

INDEX   231
```

Signification, 45
Signs, 37–38, 47
Simmel, Georg, 5
Simulation, 165–166
Snow, C. P., 198, 201–203
Social, 25, 39, 112–113
Social area analysis, 101–104
Social attitudes, 143–144
Social dimensions, *see* Attributes
Social fact, 23–24, 35, 39, 59
creation of, 186–190, 202, 206
improvement of, 193
Social philosophy, 12–13, 184, 197
Social policy, 121, 165, 202
normative and empirical theory,
177–185
applied social science, 186–195,
202
means-ends, 186–188, 190–191,
188–190, 193–195
opportunity costs in, 193
side effects of, 193
social context of, 193
Social rank, 15, 55, 130
Social science, 24, 150–151, 158–159
empirical and normative theory,
177–185
applied, 185–192, 202
uses of, 193–195
and politics, 190–191, 194
and humanities, 196–203
and ethics, 26, 203–205
and esthetics, 26, 203–206
*see also* Science
Social structure, 5–6, 23–25, 39, 56,
80–81, 100, 141
Sociology of work, 53–54, 145, 146
Solipsism, 3, 20, 22, 25, 28, 204
Space, varieties of, 99–106, 164
Space–time ratio, 100
Spatial contingency, 67, 173
Spatio-temporal continuum, 73, 78,
104, 160, 178, 184
*see also* Event
Specificity, *see* Precision
Stafford, William, 91–92
Standard men, 109–110, 115
Statistics, 97, 104–105, 171
Stimulus-response, 56
Strauss, Anselm, 55
Subjective states of mind, 25–26,

42–43, 59, 71, 110, 115
Suicide, 24–25, 122–123
Evolutionary school, 37–40
Sutherland, Edwin, 35, 118–119
Symbolization, 37–49, 64, 74, 88,
162
evolutionary view of, 37–39
Langer's view, 39–41
vs. conditioned response, 39–42
Symbols, 29–31, 37, 39, 84
psychological meaning, 42–43
logical meaning, 43–47
numerical, 126–128
Synthetic realm, 78, 158, 181
*see also* Spatio-temporal con-
tinuum
Technology, 34, 50, 53, 202
*see also* Practical vision
Temporal contingency, 67, 173
Testing, *see* Theory testing
Theory, 5, 69, 77–79, 87, 132, 142–
143, 149, 156–159, 160, 177–185,
203
defined, 123
purpose of, 122–125, 136
adequacy of, 164
elaboration of, 89, 124
grand, 158
as source of research problem,
12–13
axiomatic, 139–140
middle-range, 140
explanation, 56, 122–124, 152, 156
levels of, 154, 155
heuristic, 167
speculative, 123
*see also* Abstractive hierarchies;
Conceptual realm
Theory construction, 58, 80, 122–
124, 133–135, 140, 166–169, 171,
197
*see also* Abstractive hierarchies
Theory testing, 4, 58, 124–125, 136,
166, 169–171, 173, 197
empirical, 67, 78–79, 84, 85, 118,
119, 124, 127, 132, 134
logical, 64, 67, 84, 85, 123
*see also* Proof
Thomas, W. I., 54
Thought, 38, 41, 45–47, 71, 205
Time, 103, 120–121, 164–165, 173
```

Date Due